INVESTING IS YOUR SUPERPOWER

INVESTING

IS YOUR

Superpower

A
Step-by-Step
Guide to Creating
the Lifestyle
You've Always
Wanted

SHINOBU HINDERT, CFP®

LIONCREST
PUBLISHING

INVESTING IS YOUR SUPERPOWER
A Step-by-Step Guide to Creating the Lifestyle You've Always Wanted

ISBN   978-1-5445-1951-7 *Hardcover*
      978-1-5445-1950-0 *Paperback*
      978-1-5445-1949-4 *Ebook*

For my mom, who taught me how to break glass ceilings.

CONTENTS

INTRODUCTION

Women have been left out. In school, we learned about long division, the Pythagorean theorem, and even the rules of dodgeball. But how to effectively manage and invest our money? Nope! Didn't make the curriculum.

When you start working, you're focused on establishing your career. As you earn more money, you realize you have a variety of financial goals you want to hit. But these goals have competing priorities. How are you supposed to enjoy your life today and navigate investing for the future? What's a good investment anyway? Where do you start? So you set out on a search to get some answers.

Here's what you find.

You start talking to some friends, but it gets uncomfortable because you don't want to share all your financial details.

No problem, you think. *The internet knows everything.* So you turn to Google. You find a popular article on investing, but as you're reading, you come across a term you don't know. You open a new tab to Google that term, but then you come across something different you don't understand. Before long, you're twenty articles deep, and it feels like you know less than you did when you started. With everything buried in financial jargon, it's worse than homework.

Overwhelmed, you decide it's time to consult a professional. But then you discover you don't qualify to work with a financial advisor because you don't meet their account size minimums. You can work with a fee-only planner, but they'll charge you anywhere from $2,500 to $5,000 for a personalized plan. This plan doesn't come with free ongoing conversations or unlimited Q&A sessions, and you have plenty of questions. You try talking to your local bank but quickly get discouraged because they're immediately trying to cross-sell you products. They jump right into investment features. They don't even ask any questions about who you are and what you value.

I'm going to guess you picked up this book to try and make sense of it all. You want a clear, step-by-step roadmap to achieving ALL your financial goals. You want to move from overwhelm and confusion to clarity and confidence when choosing investments. You want to know how to pivot your financial goals when life happens. You want to automate your financial life so you can spend more time doing the things you love. But you don't know where to start. You've put in hours of work, and you've ended up in the exact place you started. Frustrated and tired of going in circles, you feel like giving up. Don't give up just yet; I promise, you are in the right place!

INVESTING IS STILL A MAN'S WORLD, BUT IT SHOULDN'T BE

In 2004, I started my first job in the financial industry at Smith

Barney, now Morgan Stanley, in one of the largest retail branches on the East Coast. Female coworkers were scarce, and I could count the number of female financial advisors on one hand. Since then, the financial industry has made intentional efforts to create diversity in the workplace. But women are far from representing half of the current financial workforce.

The industry is also enhancing its marketing and offerings to appeal to women, which is a fantastic trend, but the reality is, women have been left out of financial conversations for generations. Traditionally, men went to work and handled the money, while women served as homemakers. Although this has dramatically changed, it's been ingrained in our culture that it's rude for women to discuss money. In fact, according to a 2018 Merrill Lynch study, conducted in partnership with Age Wave, "Sixty-one percent of women would rather talk about their own death than money." Add all that up, and you have the perfect storm for leaving women behind.

On the flip side, a 2015 Fidelity Investments study revealed 92% of women want to learn more about financial planning. Despite wanting to learn more, many women don't take action because of a lack of confidence in their financial knowledge and not knowing where to turn for financial guidance.

Although change for women in finance and as investors is on the horizon, real change takes time. Do you want to wait for the industry to catch up with you, or do you want to take matters into your own hands?

Whether you're conscious of it or not, you make decisions daily based around your money. That means you are at the forefront of this cultural shift. However, change must happen within you before you can influence the larger community. As with most things in life, you need to help yourself before you can help anyone else. Flight attendants remind us every time we fly, "Please securely fasten your face mask before assisting others." In order to change the overall trends, you need to start with your own financial empowerment.

FINANCIAL EMPOWERMENT

Financial empowerment is the ability to confidently make informed decisions with your money. The side effects that come with being financially empowered? Confidence. Clarity. Freedom.

When you're financially empowered, the process of reaching all your financial goals will no longer be confusing or overwhelming. You know you can't achieve your goals overnight, but you have a clear plan for reaching them eventually. You're confident you can have the lifestyle you want, now and later, because you have an easy-to-follow plan. You can see the results on paper.

You know how to talk about money, and you know how to evaluate financial risk. Financial jargon that once made you shut off is now digestible. You are comfortable speaking with financial professionals because you know what questions to ask and how to interpret their answers. You can also effectively communicate with your friends and family and at your workplace about all things money, and you even inspire your close friends to follow in your footsteps.

Perhaps most important of all, you develop a new understanding of money. You recognize money is not your ultimate desire but a tool that allows you to freely pursue your true passions. You can confidently walk on your path to fulfillment and build a life in which you feel purpose and motivation to work each day.

With this book, your financial empowerment is my goal. I don't want you to just survive financially; I want you to *thrive*. Are you ready to jump on the path to financial empowerment?

WHAT THIS BOOK WILL TEACH YOU

In this book, you will learn how to effectively manage money to build and keep wealth without making it a full-time job. By following my three-phase process for creating your Empower Plan, you'll walk on rock-solid financial ground so you can spend time following your passions.

In Phase 1, you will build a strong financial foundation. In Phase 2, I'll introduce you to the major investment strategies and essentials you need to know. Finally, in Phase 3, you'll bring it all together in order to create your own Empower Plan and turn your goals into reality. With this Empower Plan, you will create the time, energy, and money you need to pursue what you find most important in life.

Through the course of the book, you will:

- Explore how your childhood money culture influences your financial decisions today and learn an easy-to-follow three-step process for overcoming financial roadblocks.
- Discover what you truly want from life and create clear financial goals that bring you fulfillment.
- Gain transparency on where you stand today financially.
- Break down the walls of financial jargon and build an understanding of the investing essentials everyone should know.
- Get an inside look at retirement planning and find out what all the professionals know that you were never taught.
- Make your goals reality by exploring the adjustable elements

of financial goal planning and learn how to pivot your investments as life changes.

- Set your financial life and investment strategy on autopilot so you can invest like a professional money manager without putting in hours each week.

One of the biggest challenges of any book on investing is figuring out how to translate the strategies and concepts into your daily life. To help you see how all the tips, tricks, and rules of this book play out in real life, I've created three imaginary characters. Let's meet them now.

JESSICA

Jessica is 35 years old and single with no kids. She works in medical sales for a *Fortune* 500 company. She's tall, athletic, a high achiever, and ambitious. She makes everything look so easy. You know who I'm talking about. She even looks good after running. I mean honestly, who looks good when they're covered in sweat? Jessica does. I know, I know—you already want to not like her, but she's kind to everyone. It's not possible to dislike her.

ASHLEY

Ashley is 36 years old and lives with her fiancé. They plan on getting married sometime within the next 2 years. Ashley works for a large company as a creative for a lifestyle brand. She thrives when surrounded by friends and is always trying to lift those up around her. Need a pep talk? Call Ashley. Need decorating ideas for your new place? Call Ashley. Want to whip up a meal that makes you look like a boss in the kitchen? Call Ashley. She also loves yoga and plans a wellness getaway every year. She is humble, grounded, and has a charming way about her.

MIKE AND SARAH

Mike is 37 years old, and Sarah is 34 years old. They are newlyweds and want to start planning for a baby in the next few years. Mike is self-employed as a marketing strategist. Sarah works for a 600-person women's clothing company. Both of their companies are growing fast. Sarah loves being in a high-paced environment. They are passionate about traveling and enjoy entertaining friends at their home. They tend to be opposites. Mike likes to plan everything. I bet he knows what he's eating this weekend. Sarah is a complete free spirit whose motto is "If you want it, go and get it." She is a force to be reckoned with. When her mind is made up, move over, world. Mike and Sarah bring out the best in each other. It's almost too cute.

Throughout this book, you'll follow along with Jessica, Ashley, and Mike and Sarah. You'll see how they approach common financial obstacles—or opportunities, as I like to call them—that you yourself will likely face. You'll also see what strategies they use to gain financial confidence and how they use a simplified approach to investing to get great results.

Finally, to help make things even easier, I've created a one-stop shop of digital assets, available at www.empoweredplanning.com/superpower. Here, you can find the most up-to-date resources referenced in this book and access all the worksheets, checklists, journal exercises, and other tools included throughout the book.

WHAT THIS BOOK WILL NOT TEACH YOU

There are a lot of investing books out there. I want you to know what this book is *not* because investing itself is a broad topic.

- You won't learn about alternative investments, such as Bitcoin and gold.

- You won't learn about complex investment strategies, such as shorting the markets or trading options.
- You won't learn how to become a professional financial advisor.
- You won't be getting a Personal Finance 101 breakdown, although I *will* review tips on budgeting, debt, and credit.
- You won't learn how to get rich quick.

If you're looking for any of that, this is not the book for you.

If, on the other hand, you're looking for a clear, step-by-step guide to creating and achieving multiple financial goals using a thoughtful investment strategy, you're in the right place.

WHY LISTEN TO ME?

I'm not a stuffed shirt. I'm not from a different generation. I'm not claiming to have a secret that will make you rich quick. I'm a CERTIFIED FINANCIAL PLANNER™. As an advisor, I've created personalized financial plans for hundreds of wealthy individuals and families living and spending from coast to coast. As a financial educator, I've presented more than 500 live workshops throughout Southern California covering a wide range of topics, from budgeting to estate planning. I've worked at some of the largest investment institutions, including Smith Barney (now Morgan Stanley) and Fidelity Investments.

I tell you this because I want you to know I've seen it all. I've worked with thousands of people from all walks of life. I've worked with clients who have $10 million to invest, and I've worked with recent grads with more than $100,000 in student-loan debt and no savings. I've seen the benefits of a well-executed financial plan, and I've seen the detrimental impact of financial planning being an afterthought.

With my range of experience in the financial space, I know what information and resources are available to you. What's out there isn't organized: it's buried in financial jargon and doesn't provide solutions. Through my work, I've figured out how to break down investing into simple, easy-to-understand language. I have developed a unique approach to investing that focuses on education first. This method will show you how to apply investment concepts to your real life, and it has a proven track record of success.

My goal is to simplify the complex world of investing and empower you to reach financial freedom.

You can become a savvy investor.

You can build wealth and keep it.

You can make confident financial decisions.

If you're tired of being left out of investing conversations and ready to take charge of your financial life, this book is where you start. Let's dive in!

Phase 1

Build a Foundation for Financial Empowerment

During this phase, you will:

- Understand your financial past and what role emotions play when you make financial decisions.
- Explore what you want out of life and create clear financial goals to achieve your ambitions.
- Gain transparency on what your financial life looks like today and learn how to make minor adjustments to improve your financial well-being.

CHAPTER 1

UNPACKING YOUR MONEY BAGGAGE

It's 1991. MC Hammer's "2 Legit 2 Quit" is topping the charts. *Beauty and the Beast*, *Full House*, Super Nintendo, and Cabbage Patch Kids are what I'm all about. I'm eight years old. I'm cruising the streets of northern New Jersey on my roller skates. Okay, fine, I'm not any good. The point is, I wear them in my driveway. Neighbors totally think I know how to use them.

One evening, my father asks me to sit down with him and my mom for a talk. His tone suggests a serious conversation. I sit down with purpose. In that moment, I feel like an adult. I look over at my mom; she seems nervous, which makes me nervous. My father explains to me that there are no guarantees in life. He tells me that he and my mom could die at any moment. I'm terrified. My father explains that we have no relatives living in the United States. He stresses how important it is to understand money and life. If he and my mother were to die unexpectedly, I need to know what it costs to live. He explains how much money they make versus how much they spend.

This conversation was just the beginning. Throughout my childhood, I received lessons about money, some explicit and some implicit.

My father didn't sugarcoat things. He worked long hours and usually six days a week. When we did get time together, he talked to me about his work life, money, and more. He explained the challenges and opportunities of managing a staff. He shared lessons he learned along the way. He preferred I work through situations with him, and he would guide me to form my own opinions.

My dad's reasoning for these conversations was simple. He was born and raised in Langata, Kenya, in the 1950s. Growing up in Kenya shaped my dad's belief system. He used to explain to my friends that he chose our house because it was perched on top of a hill, which allowed him to see people coming from many different angles. We had a German shepherd whose only job was to protect us from outside dangers. My father lost both of his parents before the age of eighteen. He had to become financially independent early on in life, and that stuck with him forever. He was scared to unexpectedly leave his family alone in the world. These conversations and lessons he imparted on me were his way of giving me something extra in life.

My mother grew up in Fukuoka, Japan. She was raised in an upper-middle-class family. Money was never discussed in her home. In her mind, talking to an eight-year-old girl about money was completely inappropriate, but she went along with it because she knew my father's fear was deeply rooted and not unreasonable. She couldn't guarantee tomorrow, and her family all lived in Japan and didn't speak English. My mother taught me her own lessons about money. She was the financial gatekeeper for our family, and she was like Fort Knox. She taught me the difference between wanting and needing something. Those lessons will stay with me forever.

As a kid, discussing money became a normal part of my life. The lingering fear of an impending disaster also became a normal part of my life. This fear stayed with me. It shaped my relationships with people, myself, and ultimately, money.

I have worked with hundreds of people as a financial planner and spoken with thousands as a financial educator, and they almost all had one thing in common: their childhood money cultures shaped their financial belief systems as adults. Like me and so many of the people I've worked with, you too have deeply ingrained thoughts and feelings about money because of how you were raised. It's natural to make financial decisions based on our unique emotions, so it's critical to understand your childhood money culture and the impact it has on you. When you recognize and allow space for your emotions, you can move from thinking about money to making moves with your money.

CHILDHOOD MONEY CULTURE

Have you seen those Progressive Insurance commercials about people turning into their parents? The message is, "Progressive Insurance can't stop you from becoming your parents when you buy a home, but we can protect your home and auto." It's hilarious. When I was growing up, my mom would do these annoying, smothering things. I promised myself that would never be me. I got married, had kids, and guess what? I'm her. I catch myself in these moments all the time. I overbundle my children in sixty-degree weather. I nag my husband to finish the kind-of-smelly-but-not-totally-sour leftovers I pile out of the fridge. I can see it happening in slow motion. It annoys me while I'm doing it, but I can't stop it from happening. It's safe to say, we also carry behaviors our parents had around money. We should acknowledge this.

I've shared with you the theme in my house was fear. I was afraid of being a hard-knock-life orphan. This absolutely played a role in how I treated money growing up and into my adult life. I used to hoard money I made from household chores and my first jobs. I would find a special, secret hiding spot to stash it away. Problem was, I couldn't even find it. I would literally lose cash because I was so intent on hiding it.

Everyone's experience is unique, and there are many different ways childhood money culture can show up in your life. Let's take a look at our main characters and the impacts of their childhood money cultures.

JESSICA

Money was stable in Jessica's childhood home. Her parents explained that they worked hard to provide for their children. The value of the dollar was instilled in her early on. Her father helped her open a checking account once she started babysitting neighborhood children. She remembers walking into the bank to fill out a deposit slip. This made her proud.

Jessica's mom thought it was impolite for Jessica to talk about money. She told Jessica to focus on schoolwork and being a kid. Her mother treated money like it was a private matter, and this stayed with Jessica into her adult life.

Today, Jessica wants to learn more about investing. She's saving money, as she was taught to do as a child, but she doesn't know if she's saving enough. She knows strategies exist to leverage her money. She doesn't know how to get started, though, and she feels uncomfortable talking about her finances with other people.

ASHLEY

Ashley grew up the child of a single mom. She saw her mother struggle financially. Her mom was bitter about not having money. When Ashley would ask for toys or new clothes, her mom made it clear those were reserved for rich people.

Today, Ashley wants to start looking at money through a new lens. She is confidently living within her means but isn't sure how to merge finances with her future hubby. The idea of having to share her money is bringing up a lot of insecurities, doubts, and questions.

MIKE AND SARAH

Sarah's dad worked a mid-level management job and did all the right things financially. He worked hard to provide for his family. He made saving a priority and often sacrificed things for himself, such as an updated wardrobe or new car, so he could save for retirement and put money into a rainy day fund for the family. Unfortunately, he died when Sarah was twelve years old. Sarah feels like her dad didn't get to live the life he wanted. As a result, she'd rather spend money on experiences and things she enjoys now than save it for a day that may never come.

When Mike was a child, his parents fought about money all the time. Mike was aware they were poor. He never invited his friends over because he was embarrassed of everything they didn't have. He also didn't want his friends to hear his parents fighting. Now, discussions about money make him nervous, and he often worries about not having enough.

Today, Mike and Sarah want to get on the same page with how they think about money. They are ready to pave a new path for their future, but money is a point of stress for them.

By now, hopefully you can see how childhood money culture can have a big influence on a person's belief system around money. In exploring the money culture of your own childhood home, it's not about undoing all that you've learned but understanding what impact that belief system has on the decisions you make today.

> **Empowered Planning Golden Rule:** Acknowledge the past, embrace it for the lessons it taught you, and release whatever doesn't serve you anymore.

JOURNAL EXERCISE

Now it's your turn! Take some time to explore your own childhood money culture and see what comes up. This is a judgment-free zone. Some things may make you uncomfortable, but try to avoid casting judgments such as "My parents had no idea what they were doing" or "I'll never be good at this." You're not trying to solve anything right now. Just explore and observe.

Here are some questions to get the juices flowing:

- What was the language or culture in your home growing up around money?
- What were the positive things you learned?
- What are some things you'd like to do differently?

If it's safe and comfortable to do so, call your parents or mentors. Ask them to share their financial wins over the years. Ask them about their mistakes. Be ready to be vulnerable as well. Share what you're doing right now to improve your financial wellness.

YOUR FINANCIAL DECISIONS MIGHT NOT BE AS LOGICAL AS YOU THINK

When it comes to our finances, making logical decisions is almost always our intention. We plan to weigh the benefits and limitations of a specific financial decision, explore the immediate and long-term impacts, and then make the decision logically. But it's easy to let our gut feeling dictate what path we ultimately take— often without even realizing what's happening. In fact, there's a whole field of study, behavioral finance, dedicated to how our psychology influences financial decisions. Behavioral finance suggests our natural biases can lead us to make illogical or irrational financial decisions.

Here's an example: Greg is selling his home for $1 million. He will not accept an offer he received for $980,000, instead letting the house sit on the market for months and months. A $20,000 reduction is only a 2% difference between what he is asking and the offer. Logically, this decision doesn't make a lot of sense, but to Greg, this is more than a house. This home is the epicenter of the happiest years of his life. He's attached an emotional value that drives his decision.

We're not perfect; we're real! As much as we want to make financial decisions logically, it's hard to separate ourselves from our emotions. Trying to ignore our emotions and their impact doesn't work. We must instead become aware of our emotions. Many emotions affect our financial decisions, but the far most prevalent one I see is fear. Keep reading and see if any of this resonates with you. If so, your financial decisions are probably not as logical as you'd like right now. But don't worry, in the next chapter, we'll work through what to do with all our emotional baggage .

FEAR IS A POWERFUL DRIVER

Fear is triggered in us anytime we perceive a threat, whether it's real or imagined. As I was getting ready to give birth to my son, the topic of fear was brought up on a regular basis. I was repeatedly told by women in the birthing community that I needed to learn how to relax into a contraction. They said if I physically tightened up, my body would respond to this fear as indicating a possible threat. This could potentially stop labor. Say what? Let me get this straight: I have to experience the most intense pain I've ever felt and just chill while it's happening? Sit back and imagine myself getting a foot rub? It blew my mind that reacting to pain could trigger my survival instincts—that my body would assume I was about to be attacked by a grizzly bear and stop labor.

Emotional fear has real consequences. We make decisions based on "gut" feelings all the time. How many times have you said no to a second date because you had a bad gut feeling about the person? Our gut instincts can warn us of real danger. When it comes to our finances and investing, though, following our gut can be problematic. Fear around money can manifest in many ways, but two of the most common are *avoidance* and *inaction*.

AVOIDANCE

When you are afraid of what you'll find, you often discover it's much easier to avoid or ignore certain things. This is also known as the ostrich effect: you bury your head in the sand. Here's an example: You want to start investing. You don't know where or how to start. You do some research online. Your heart rate picks up and overwhelm hits you. You close your laptop, telling yourself you'll do it later. You revisit the subject three months later, and the same thing happens. Each time you close your laptop, your anxiety goes away. In that moment, you subconsciously tell yourself, "When I avoid learning about investing, I become calm." This reinforces your avoidance behavior. You sabotage your goals because you don't want to feel uncomfortable. The more you avoid anxiety-driven situations, the more you will continue to do so in the future.

Avoidance is how Ashley's fear manifests. She has a lot of anxiety about money because of her upbringing. She's explored financial education in the past, but it brought up all her old anxieties, and she was quickly overwhelmed. She finds it easier to ignore the subject altogether.

Avoidance can also show up as escapism. Most of the time, escapism comes with optimism or blind faith. Escapism tends to show up as a stress-coping strategy for many couples. Rather than knowingly get into a disagreement about money, ignoring financial issues helps keep the peace. For example, Sarah gets out of having spending conversations with Mike through escapism. She assures him everything will work out, and her blind faith and optimism make it difficult for Mike to have candid conversations about their money. Mike also uses escapism as a strategy to avoid discussing their finances. Since their money conversations heat up quickly, Mike has started to ignore their finances because he doesn't want to pick a fight with Sarah. Being agreeable and escaping conversations that cause stress in their relationship have become their default solutions.

INACTION

Sometimes fear manifests as inaction because of our innate desire to avoid regrets in life. In this case, inertia can act as a barrier to making financial decisions. Afraid of making a mistake, we take no action at all. For example, I have a friend, Jody, who seriously researches everything. She's always exploring. For the last couple of years, each January she's declared that year as her Year of Money. Each year, nothing happens. She researches and explores until she has informational paralysis. She doesn't want to make the "wrong" decision, and not making any decision at all is an easy solution.

Jessica struggles with inaction. She's something of a perfectionist and is used to being a high achiever. She doesn't want to make a mistake, so she can't bring herself to make a decision.

FACING YOUR FEARS

If you let fear dictate your decisions, you won't be able to make the smartest moves with your money. The best antidote to fear? Education. The more you understand your finances, the less you'll fear them. We make logical decisions with our money when we approach it from a place of power, confidence, or authority. This is possible, and reading this book is a giant step in the right direction.

Even with education, sometimes you will need to work *through* your fear. Take baby steps. The goal is to create a lifestyle you want that's supported by your money. Working with your money isn't a one-and-done task.

If your fear shows up as avoidance, take steps to alleviate your anxiety. Create a serene and calm setting as you dig into your finances. Dust off your oil diffuser, throw in a dash of lavender, and fill up the room with calming smells.

When you talk to your partner about money, take a walk in nature to kick off the discussion. Be respectful and look at it as an opportunity to grow as a couple and get to know each other on a deeper level. Listen before you talk. Set a time limit; I recommend no more than one hour. With work, you'll find talking about money can actually bring you closer together.

If your fear shows up as inaction, understand that not making a decision is making a decision to do nothing, and that's a mistake. Hope is not a plan. It's far better to take control of your financial future than leave it to fate. You might not make the perfect decision, and that's okay. In this book, I'll guide you through the best practices for making financial decisions so you can have confidence in your judgment.

Whether you're planning alone or with a partner, anytime you sit down and work with your money, treat yourself to a reward afterward. Maybe you go out for chocolate gelato (yummy yummy). Or maybe shots of tequila. It's your call. You need to practice self-care so planning with your money becomes routine and the attendant anxiety decreases each time.

JOURNAL EXERCISE

Now it's your turn! Explore some previous decisions you've made with your money. Identify what emotional drivers were at play. Remember, this is a judgment-free zone.

Here are some questions to get the juices flowing:

- What were the last three financial decisions you made, and how did you make them?
- What are three money moves you've been thinking about making, and what's been holding you back (e.g., lack of time, lack of information)?
- When you read the section on money fears, what came up?
- What areas of this section spoke to you the most and why?
- What areas of this section do you think you're unaffected by and why?
- What are some things you'd like to change about how you make financial decisions? (The answer could be as simple as "Actually make a decision.")

KEY TAKEAWAYS

In this chapter, we explored how our childhood money culture influences our belief system today and how our emotions, particularly fear, can dictate how we make financial decisions.

The journal exercises you went through in this chapter should have brought out some powerful emotions but not with the intention of holding you there. Remember the Empowered Planning Golden Rule: Acknowledge the past, embrace it for the lessons it taught you, and release whatever doesn't serve you anymore.

If this chapter brought up too much and you're spinning, call a friend to chat. If you feel like you can't move forward from here because there's too much to digest, explore one-on-one therapy. You're on your way to a breakthrough, so keep the momentum going!

But if you're ready to keep going, now what? It's time to look deeper at how your childhood money culture and emotional views of money have led to money blind spots. In the next chapter, we'll look at the most common money blind spots and explore a three-step process for transforming your money mindset.

CHAPTER 2

TRANSFORMING YOUR MONEY MINDSET

In my early adulthood, I was on the right financial track. On paper, it looked like I had it all figured out. More was happening behind the scenes, though. "No" was my motto. Take a trip with some girlfriends for the weekend? No, I can't. Buy that new outfit I've been eyeing? No, I can't. I missed out on countless adventures with friends. I even missed my best friend's bachelorette party. I was the maid of honor! But I couldn't bring myself to spend money on a flight back to the East Coast. To be clear, I had the money; I just couldn't bring myself to spend it. I'm not proud of that.

I was suffering from a money blind spot. A money blind spot is a mindset that obstructs the way we view money in our lives, and guess what? We all have them. My big money blind spot is scarcity. I've had to intentionally learn how to find the balance between my gut instinct to hoard money and my need to live life. I've had to work on erasing the fear that everything can go to pieces tomorrow. I've learned to tear down the barriers I set up between me and everyone else. This has been a freeing experience but not something I was able to change overnight.

Too often, people make the mistake of focusing on a single financial issue rather than seeking the holistic view of their money mindset. For example, you can become so focused on creating the perfect budget or saving "enough" money to invest, you don't realize your money blind spot is deterring you from pursuing your ultimate goals. This is why addressing one's emotional relationship with money is the first part of Empowered Academy, my ten-week, live training course, and the first thing I do in one-on-one work with clients.

Emotional roadblocks will pop up throughout your financial journey. They may not be top of mind today. They may not be driving every decision you make. But your money blind spots *will* come up on your path to reaching your financial goals. Rather than push ahead, only to come to a halting stop later, it's important to transform your money mindset up front. There's no point in hiding from your money blind spots. They always come back.

In this chapter, I will detail six of the most common money blind spots and teach you an easy three-step process to work through your emotional roadblocks and transform your money mindset.

DISCOVER YOUR MONEY BLIND SPOTS

Having an abundant mindset around money is the ultimate goal. This is when you feel like there's more than enough for everyone. Other people making money doesn't present itself as a threat to you or your happiness. You move through each day with confidence because you know the lifestyle you want is waiting for you to create it. You look at money challenges as opportunities. You own the fact that you're responsible for where you go in life. You don't walk; you strut.

When it comes to your money blind spots, you may be totally

unaware of them, or maybe you're aware of them but choose to ignore them. When left unchallenged, your money blind spots become habitual and part of your everyday thinking. We all have this inside-head voice that talks to us throughout the day. Sometimes this voice is our best friend, and other times, she's a complete frenemy. The stories she tells us can become roadblocks to achieving what we want in life. This is especially true with money.

To normalize these inside-head voices, I've named mine Sulky Suzie and Drama Queen Jolene. Sulky Suzie is my limiting belief system. Drama Queen Jolene is my fear and anxiety. I highly recommend you name your inside-head voices, too. Maybe you have a Sulky Suzie, like me; or perhaps a Mediocre Molly, encouraging you to settle for less than you really want; or a Judgy Jane, who makes you feel ashamed about your finances. Personalizing your inside-head voice makes it more approachable. You will start to have fun. Trust me.

Sulky Suzie or Drama Queen Jolene come around when I face challenges (which are opportunities in disguise). They cast doubt and make me second guess myself. They are not women I would choose to be friends with. Imagine you tell your friend you're exploring your money culture. You share that you're starting to doubt whether you can achieve what you've set out to accomplish, and her response is, "Well, yeah. You really can't have what you want. That's life." Is that the kind of person you want to be friends with? Nope.

We don't accept this kind of behavior from our friends, so why would we accept it from ourselves? When your downer inside-head voice pokes her head out, simply say, "Sorry, Sulky Suzie, not today." Move on because ain't nobody got time for that. For real. You're juggling a lot. You don't need to spend time listening to someone you wouldn't even be friends with! Truth bomb.

Discovering your blind spots is not about being perfect. It's not about having good or bad thoughts about money. It's about identifying what role your emotions play in your decisions and how to recognize when they're hurting your financial well-being.

JOURNAL EXERCISE

Now it's your turn! Write down what story or stories you've been telling yourself about money. What's Sulky Suzie reminding you of every day? Here are some prompts to get the juices flowing:

- When I think about money I...
- I feel stuck when I try to create money goals because...
- I haven't taken more action with my money because...
- When I see people who have the lifestyle I want, I feel...
- When I look at my account balances, I feel...

SIX COMMON MONEY BLIND SPOTS

The things your Sulky Suzie or Drama Queen Jolene says will be unique to you, but there are some common patterns I've identified through my work. There are six common money blind spots I come across again and again: complacency, shame, damsel in distress, scarcity, victim, and overconfidence. These words are meant to be powerful. If they evoke emotion, understand that's the whole point. We'll explore them to get through to the other side. There's no right or wrong, good or bad. This is a judgment-free zone.

COMPLACENCY

Complacency leaves you overly content with your current situation. When you are complacent, you aren't thriving, but you're also not depressed. You want to improve your financial well-being, but you have trouble finding the motivation. You can be easily overwhelmed. You don't know where to start.

The fascinating part about complacency is that it can be a form of self-sabotage. You choose not to go after your dreams because deep down, you don't think you deserve to have them. Mind-blowing right? You write your goals on your to-do list but never end up taking action to achieve them.

An example of this is my client Melissa. By the time we started working together, she admitted she had been wanting to get on top of her finances for over two years. Professional accountability was a priority for Melissa because of her complacency blind spot. She needed directive guidance on how to get started planning for all her goals.

SHAME

Shame! Don't you just picture Cersei in *Game of Thrones* walking back to the Red Keep? It's an intense scene in many ways. This is an accurate depiction of how we feel shame internally. For so long, even talking about money was considered distasteful and rude. With this kind of culture, what happens when we make financial mistakes? We naturally internalize them. We begin to believe the untrue stories we tell ourselves.

From the thousands of people I've worked with over the years, I've learned shame comes in many different shapes and sizes. I've met clients who feel shame around having money; they feel guilty about their accomplishments. I have clients who feel shame about not having enough money and are embarrassed by their perceived poverty. I've met clients who feel shame about making financial mistakes, such as buying an investment that didn't pan out, purchasing a home that didn't appreciate, taking on too much debt, and the list goes on.

DAMSEL IN DISTRESS

Okay, so this title is a little dramatic. I don't know many women who are hanging out in castles, brushing their hair all day, and waiting for their knight in shining armor to appear. But I do see a more subtle version that is all too common. Many women I've worked with admit this money blind spot to me after a few meetings. It's not something they wear as a badge of honor, but it's something they've discovered through self-work. They have this aha moment where they realize they've actually been waiting for someone else to take care of their finances for them.

An example of this is my client Amanda. She always viewed money as being a masculine trait. She thought it was something men just knew how to do. She also never talked about money with her friends. She thought it would be rude and tacky for her to bring it up. When she finally met her knight in shining armor, he was swimming in debt from switching master's degree programs. Up until this point, Amanda had been an independent, self-sufficient woman with a good understanding of her financial picture. She never took it further, though, because the seed had been planted in her mind that she didn't need to learn about investing or plan out her financial goals. Someone else would take care of it for her, right? It wasn't an intentional thought. It was background noise that was dictating her decision. Once she realized her knight in shining armor *wasn't* going to take care of it for her, she was determined to take control of her own financial empowerment.

SCARCITY

Viewing money through a scarcity lens makes you believe you never have enough. There are two main camps within the scarcity mindset. The first group spends money as quickly as they get it, thinking if they don't spend it now, it'll be gone in the future. The second group (which I've been a part of before) hoards money. Doing this makes them feel secure since they're certain they'll run out of money in the future. People with a scarcity mindset run the gamut. We're talking about people with more money in their accounts than they could ever spend in a lifetime to people with nothing more than a few dollars in their pockets.

There's a feeling of lack that follows you around with a scarcity mindset. You are constantly searching for evidence to feed Sulky Suzie. "I have debt. Sulky Suzie is right; I don't have enough money." "My income is going up, but so are my income taxes. Sulky Suzie is right; I need more money." The scarcity mindset can also be an unhealthy motivator. When you consistently think you need more money, you aren't able to fully celebrate your accomplishments. The scarcity mindset can also manifest itself in feeling jealous of friends when they have financial success. And then you feel like crap because you're a crappy friend. Don't worry, we're going to change all of that.

VICTIM

Feeling like a victim helps you avoid taking responsibility for your actions. "It's not *my* fault. It's the government/corporate America/ the education system/my parents…"—the list goes on. This is the harshest but simplest way to look at it.

The truth is, many of you were simply doing what you were told. Take on debt so you can pay for school. Use this credit card so you can have it now. The public school system in the United States doesn't offer formalized education around finances. Working through the victim mentality doesn't mean your experiences weren't real. Your experiences are part of you, but they are not *who* you are. We can't change yesterday, only prepare for tomorrow.

My coworker Monica went through a period where she felt victimized by our employer. She never had a lot of money left over at the end of the month. According to Monica, it was the company's fault. After all, it was a big company. They paid executives millions of dollars. Monica went through life with this bitter attitude. She felt helpless in fighting "the system." I tried to talk to her about higher-paying opportunities inside and outside the company. Her rationale for not exploring them was laden with excuses. I also tried to talk to her about getting a roommate to make her rent more manageable. My efforts fell on deaf ears. She wasn't ready to take responsibility for where she was financially in life. She was holding herself back from thriving.

The victim mentality is particularly dangerous because it can be contagious and become a competition. Remember that scene in *Mean Girls*, the one where they're standing around talking about what they hate about their bodies? If you surround yourself with people who feel sorry for themselves, you begin to chime in. So choose your friends wisely.

OVERCONFIDENCE

In general, it's said people have an inflated view of their own abilities. Everyone but me. I don't do that. *wink wink* This tendency isn't all bad. It shows people tend to view the world in positive terms. The tricky part is when this inflated view spills over into how you make decisions with your money. Overconfidence then becomes a blind spot.

Overconfidence is directly linked to an inflated, false sense of control. You think everything will work out with your money goals, and you refuse to listen to anyone. Overconfidence can show up as taking on too much risk with your money. Oftentimes, you also can't see financial mistakes you've made.

My neighbor Karen is an extreme example of overconfidence. She was always chasing these hot new investments. Because I work in the industry, she constantly wanted me to look into them for her. I would do some research and share information I found that illustrated the unnecessary risks involved in these investments. Each time, she would dismiss my findings and tell me, "Well, that's not what I was told. I did my research, too, and it looks really good." She would often lose a lot of money in these investments, but she focused solely on her rare wins. When an investment would do well, she would brag about what a savvy investor she was, even though in total, she'd lost more money than she'd gained. Karen's overconfidence that she could predict the future growth of her investments and her lack of ability to reflect on her financial mistakes were dangerous. She and her husband ultimately separated their accounts so Karen wouldn't risk money they were relying on to meet their goals.

Right now, you might not be suffering from overconfidence, but as you begin investing and have early wins, your confidence will grow. That's a good thing. Just be wary of *over*confidence.

Empowered Planning Golden Rule: The side effects of understanding your money blind spots are freedom and creativity.

MONEY BLIND SPOTS IN ACTION

These money blind spots show up in different ways in all of us. Your childhood money culture tends to have a big influence on which blind spots you develop and how they manifest, but your blind spots also evolve depending on your experiences and where you are in life. It's also very common to have more than just one blind spot. Let's take a look at examples from our main characters.

JESSICA'S MONEY BLIND SPOTS: SHAME, DAMSEL IN DISTRESS

Talking about money makes Jessica uncomfortable. Her first reaction is embarrassment. She gets physically tense when she thinks a conversation is heading toward money. This is quickly followed by shame that she doesn't have it all figured out. Jessica feels like she's been successful in so many areas of her life; why doesn't she just get this stuff? She's been winging it. She doesn't want to make any mistakes. She's secretly hoping someone else will take care of it for her.

ASHLEY'S MONEY BLIND SPOTS: VICTIM, COMPLACENCY

Talking about money brings up resentment Ashley has toward her mother. She wishes her mother handled things differently when she was a child. Ashley feels like the stock market is reserved for wealthy people. She also believes that because she's a creative person, she will never be good at investing. She isn't good at math, and the world of finance intimidates her. Ashley's a little frustrated she's not where she thought she'd be in life at her age, but she also isn't having money problems. So she figures, why bother going down that road?

MIKE AND SARAH'S MONEY BLIND SPOTS: SCARCITY, OVERCONFIDENCE

Mike and Sarah both have a scarcity blind spot but in opposite ways. Mike grew up with money being scarce, and as a result, he hoards it today. He keeps a lot of cash in the bank and at his home with Sarah. He's afraid to take financial risk and hates debt. He gets anxious thinking about Sarah's student loans and how freely she spends money.

In contrast, Sarah lives for today. She gets overwhelmed with planning and anxiety at the idea of having to decrease her current spending. She has so much she wants to do with her life, and she loves her lifestyle. She knows her debt and how she treats money is causing tension between her and Mike, but she doesn't know what tomorrow will bring. She'd rather spend her money now and enjoy her life. She's afraid if she doesn't spend her money now, she'll never get the chance to enjoy it.

Sarah also suffers from overconfidence. She pays the minimums toward her student loans and doesn't have any other debt. She thinks she's doing okay and believes everything will work out in the end.

Money blind spots are totally normal. We'll use them as building blocks to create a positive money mindset. Once you understand your starting point, you can reframe your thinking and create a clear path to take giant steps forward.

OVERCOMING YOUR MONEY BLIND SPOTS

Now that you understand your money blind spots, you can create a system to overcome them. These blind spots often pop up when you are on the edge of getting to the next level of your financial goals. They show up as a gut feeling or that little inside-head voice that holds you back. Let that be a light bulb that you're facing a money blind spot you need to overcome. Here are three easy steps you can use to transform your money mindset when you hit roadblocks:

1. Acknowledge the thought
2. Reframe your thinking
3. Move through it

ACKNOWLEDGE THE THOUGHT

Acknowledging your money blind spots and emotional biases is key. Ignoring them will guarantee their inevitable return. Remember, we all have them. You are not alone. Since they're in your head, they know where you live. They will find you. You want to acknowledge the money blind spot or bias as it comes up.

Here's an example: You're about to make a career-change decision. You're feeling pumped, ready to write your resignation letter, and suddenly, there's a knock at the door. It's Sulky Suzie carrying suitcases. She needs a place to crash for a few weeks. Slamming the door in her face is avoidance. She will come back. Instead, you can say hello and invite her in for refreshments. You two have a short chat, then you politely ask her to leave. You don't start clearing out your kid's bedroom so Sulky Suzie can crash on the top bunk. You're looking these fears in the face. You're saying, "I know you're here. I have important things to do, so you can't stick around."

REFRAME YOUR THINKING

Reframing your thinking is an important part of this process. You want to remind yourself of what's true. The limiting beliefs, doubts, or fears are real feelings, but they're not true. Reframe the story you're telling yourself into positive, true statements.

MOVE THROUGH IT

You can move through these mindset blocks by creating realistic solutions. Creating positive solutions for your money blind spots and emotional biases allows you to make sound decisions. Then, instead of getting stuck in the same old patterns, you can move forward to the new mindset and behaviors you want.

Let's take a look at some examples of how this three-step process works. I've included suggested solutions, but as you practice this technique, you will find your own unique solutions that work best for you.

Money Blind Spot: Complacency
Step 1—Acknowledge the Thought

The MYTHS you tell yourself:

- I'm happy with my current financial picture.
- I don't have time.
- I'm not rich, and I need more money before I start planning for my future.

These things are FALSE!

Step 2—Reframe Your Thinking

The TRUTH is:

- Improving my financial well-being will open up options and give me the freedom of choice. I am worth it!
- It is worth finding the time to seek happiness and fulfillment in my life.
- I have enough money to begin planning for my future. The sooner I start, the sooner I'll reach my goals.

Step 3—Move through It

One SOLUTION: accountability. Maybe you can do this yourself by using calendar reminders, or maybe you need to hire a professional. Only you know what's right for you. But doing nothing and kicking the can down the road doesn't work. You need accountability.

Money Blind Spot: Shame
Step 1—Acknowledge the Thought

The MYTHS you tell yourself:

- It's embarrassing I don't know more.
- I shouldn't have taken on this much debt—I'm such a screw-up!

These things are FALSE!

Step 2—Reframe Your Thinking

The TRUTH is:

- I can learn from my past.
- I'm not perfect; I'm real.

Step 3—Move through It

One SOLUTION: open up to people who will support you. Having community discussions around financial shame will show you you're not alone. We can all learn from each other, and this will help you let your guard down and begin to heal from the shame you may feel internally.

Money Blind Spot: Damsel in Distress
Step 1—Acknowledge the Thought

The MYTH you tell yourself:

- Someone else will take care of my finances for me.

MAYBE, but why risk it?

Step 2—Reframe Your Thinking

The TRUTH is:

- I own my future.
- I am in control of my money.
- I am the best possible person to plan and achieve my financial goals.

Step 3—Move through It

One SOLUTION: raise your financial awareness. Take baby steps. Picking up this book puts you on the right path.

Money Blind Spot: Scarcity
Step 1—Acknowledge the Thought

The MYTH you tell yourself:

- I'll never have enough money.

This is FALSE!

Step 2—Reframe Your Thinking

The TRUTH is:

- I can have the lifestyle I've always wanted but thought I couldn't afford.
- I look around and see money all around me. There's enough out there for me!

Step 3—Move through It

One SOLUTION: abundance affirmations. Cheesy? Well, that depends on who you ask, but they work! Pick one you like and make it your money motto. Here's an example: "Money comes to me in expected and unexpected ways." Print your affirmation on a Post-it and attach it to your mirror, dashboard, laptop, or refrigerator. Don't bother tearing it down when friends come over. If they ask what it's all about, be honest. It could help the person you least expect. Besides, you're about to be rich; they'll totally want to know your secret.

Money Blind Spot: Victim
Step 1—Acknowledge the Thought

The MYTHS you tell yourself:

- It's somebody else's fault I'm not where I should or want to be.
- It's somebody else's fault I don't have the money I need or want.

These are FALSE!

Step 2—Reframe Your Thinking
The TRUTH is:

- I own my future.
- I am in control of my money.

Step 3—Move through It

One SOLUTION: forgiveness. Maybe you can do this on your own, or maybe it's time you embrace therapy. Forgive those people and experiences that have brought you pain and limiting beliefs about what you can achieve in life. You can have the lifestyle you want. It's yours to have. Forgiveness doesn't mean you have to forget, but you're worth changing for. Remove the internal roadblocks that hold you back. Shout it out loud, "Sorry, Sulky Suzie, not today!"

Money Blind Spot: Overconfidence
Step 1—Acknowledge the Thought

The MYTH you tell yourself:

- I don't need any help; I know what I'm doing. I got this.

This is FALSE!

Step 2—Reframe Your Thinking

The TRUTH is:

- There are so many resources available for me to bounce my ideas off.
- I will welcome input before making decisions.

Step 3—Move through It

One SOLUTION: work with a reputable professional. Your emotions run high, and if you get an idea in your head, it's tough to shake it loose. You need unbiased, sound advice from someone who isn't afraid to shoot you straight. This will serve as a reminder to evaluate possible outcomes before you execute any ideas.

DON'T WAIT UNTIL YOU HIT A ROADBLOCK

I want you to apply this three-step process—acknowledge the thought, reframe your thinking, and move through it—to all your blind spots. Don't wait until you hit a roadblock. Do it now; write it all down. I'm not under the false pretense that you can fix your money mindset by simply writing sentences, but I want you to have a plan for overcoming Sulky Suzie and Drama Queen Jolene when they rear their bitter heads.

You never know when you'll come across an internal roadblock. We can't eliminate the unexpected, but we can prepare for how we deal with it. Remember fire drills as a kid in school? You practiced lining up and walking out of the school to a safe zone, then there was a roll call. Schools do this to be prepared. They don't plan on having fires, but they have safety measures in place and take preventative actions so that in the event of an emergency, everyone knows what to do.

This is the same thing. The solutions you come up with now will prevent you from spiraling or making knee-jerk reactions in the future. When you start that negative self-talk or your heart rate begins to increase while confronting money challenges (oopsie, I mean opportunities), you can refer back to this work. You can follow your plan for getting through the roadblock and keep moving toward your goals.

KEY TAKEAWAYS

In this chapter, we talked about our limiting belief systems and met Sulky Suzie and Drama Queen Jolene to personalize these behaviors. We also reviewed six common money blind spots: complacency, shame, damsel in distress, scarcity, victim, and overconfidence.

We got our second Empowered Planning Golden Rule: The side effects of understanding your money blind spots are freedom and creativity. Acknowledging your money blind spots clears roadblocks that hold you back financially and sends you on your way to reaching your money goals.

Since life isn't all unicorns and rainbows, we reviewed a three-step process for transforming your money mindset when blind spots appear or your outlook needs adjusting: acknowledge the thought, reframe your thinking, and move through it. In the journal exercises, you practiced this process and created solutions to emotional roadblocks so when they come up in the future, you have a plan.

Phew! Take a deep breath! Now that you've said "Hello" and "See you later" to your money blind spots, we can move on to the fun part. Going forward, you can really get creative and think deeply and clearly about the kind of lifestyle you want for yourself.

CHAPTER 3

EXPLORING THE POSSIBLE

Picture yourself at age 60. You've been asked to be the keynote speaker at a women's empowerment conference. You're being honored with a leadership achievement award for the trail you blazed in your field and as an influential mentor for aspiring women. The venue is a new outdoor garden space with round, white tablecloths. Vases overflow with hydrangeas at the center of each table. It's sunny, the birds are chirping, you feel a cool breeze flow through your hair. You step up to the podium. You look out at the young women in the audience, who eagerly stare back at you; to them, you have all the answers. You breathe deep, taking the moment in. This is where you envisioned yourself years ago. You smile and say, "Thank you for presenting me with this award. I am humbled by the recognition. I am grateful that I have been able to lead a life of fulfillment." Only you know what the rest of the speech contains.

Life is not a dress rehearsal. This is the real deal. In this chapter, I'll challenge you to think about what you want out of life—what do you want to say in that speech? We'll explore what financial freedom means to you, what your goals are, and why you value what you do. Once you understand what you want, financial planning becomes part of your lifestyle. It will no longer be a forced, uncomfortable task.

DON'T SETTLE FOR PLAN B

When I first meet potential clients, they are typically working on their backup plan, Plan B, because they unintentionally dismiss their ability to have Plan A.

Let's look at Jessica as an example of how we can unintentionally be working toward Plan B. Jessica is in good financial shape. She is living comfortably. She's had her head down, working, establishing herself in her career, and enjoying her day-to-day life. She doesn't have any major issues that need to be addressed. She is interested in leveraging her money and maximizing the resources she has available, but she has no idea how. Without a working knowledge of investing, she has been winging it with her finances and hasn't been intentionally working toward a specific goal. She doesn't know what's possible. She thinks about buying a home, getting a new car, and investing in the stock market. Overwhelm quickly follows, making it easy to move financial planning to the back burner.

Jessica has been unintentionally settling for Plan B because she hasn't taken the time to define what her Plan A is. This is very common. Most people's Plan A is jumbled in their head. As a result, they settle into their comfort zone, which is Plan B.

Another reason we settle for Plan B is because emotions and money blind spots pop up when we begin thinking about our financial goals. One funny hiccup that gets in the way is thinking your plan needs to be perfect or precise. It feels final. You don't want to make a mistake and start planning for the "wrong" goal. Guess what? That's Drama Queen Jolene disguising herself as fear. If you find yourself taking goal planning too seriously, you're doing it wrong. This is where you get to dream up what you want for your life.

Many women I work with get overwhelmed when they start thinking about their financial goals because there are so many. They tell themselves they can't achieve them all. If you're thinking, "Okay, Shinobu, I can't have WHATEVER I want," I would say, "Tell Sulky Suzie to pack her bags and leave town!" How do you know you can't have what you want? Have you checked out a dialed-in plan to get it?

Luckily, you have a plan for any money blind spots or limiting thoughts that arise. Remember the three-step process from the last chapter: acknowledge the thought, reframe your thinking, and move through it.

All that said, this isn't a foofoo fluffy unicorn and rainbows book. I'm not saying create unrealistic goals. If you currently don't have any retirement savings, it's unreasonable to set a goal of being completely retired in 5 years, living in a luxury high-rise in New York City, and vacationing at your château in Paris. Sipping cocktails on the private island you own is probably out of reach. Unless it isn't. Then, yes, I'm free to hang out. Can you have a cold, eucalyptus-scented towel available when I deboard the private jet? I'll need that after a long flight.

But seriously, I want you to create a realistic but ambitious Plan A that you can achieve based on the resources available to you.

Screw Plan B! Let's go after Plan A. Leave your backup plan in the dust.

WHAT DOES FINANCIAL FREEDOM MEAN TO YOU?

In general, financial freedom means having enough savings, investments, and cash on hand to afford the life you want. Personalize this definition to what you want and be open to the possibility that it can mean something different to your partner. For you, financial freedom might mean having options, the ability to leverage your money, or a comfortable retirement. To me, financial freedom is having financial security. I want the peace of mind of knowing I can do the things I want to do today without compromising what I want for my future.

Let's look at what financial freedom means to our main characters.

JESSICA

Financial freedom to Jessica is having clarity. Jessica wants certainty that she is planning with purpose. Up until now, she's being doing all the right things. She has savings and a 401(k), but she's been winging it. She wants clarity on what she needs to do next. She wants to know why she should do it. What's the outcome she should expect?

ASHLEY

For Ashley, financial freedom is having options without sacrifice. Since Ashley grew up without a lot of the extras, she's intentional about providing for herself as an adult. She wants to enjoy her life but doesn't know if this means she can't reach her other goals, like saving for a down payment on a home, having a cushion to help her mother live comfortably, saving for retirement, and more.

MIKE AND SARAH

Mike's version of financial freedom is security. He wants to be free to enjoy today and build for the future. Right now, he has a pit in his stomach that they're neglecting crucial elements of their financial stability.

Sarah's version of financial freedom means flexibility. She wants to have the freedom to change her mind. She doesn't want to feel restricted. She understands the idea of financial planning, but she also knows you can't guarantee tomorrow.

JOURNAL EXERCISE

Now it's your turn! Here are some prompts to get the creative juices flowing:

- The first thing that comes to mind when I think of financial freedom is...
- My version of financial freedom is _____ because ___(why)___ .
- I used to think financial planning was only for _____, but now I realize I can benefit from financial planning because _____.
- What concerns come to mind when you think about how to financially plan for all the things you want? Be as specific as you can.

IDENTIFY YOUR SPECIFIC GOALS

Once you know what financial freedom means to you, you can begin identifying your goals. It's important to be specific and separate your various goals.

Here's why: Imagine you are fancy and have fancy friends. You volunteer to host a dinner party for ten people. You have five courses you need to make, all with different ingredients, different cooking temperatures, and different cook times. If you throw all your ingredients on the counter together and wing it, things aren't going to turn out well. You might end up with undercooked fish as your main course, and you might accidentally use salt instead of sugar in your pudding. Ew. In order to throw a hit dinner party, you need to focus on each dish individually, organizing the ingredients accordingly and planning out when everything needs to go into the oven or onto the stove.

This same principle applies to creating financial goals. When you don't clearly separate your money goals, it gets messy. All the ingredients get mixed together, making it difficult to reach a particular goal. The solution? Separate your goals into buckets based on the time frame for when you'll use the money, and give them each a fun, inspiring nickname. This will spark your motivation each time you pull up your accounts and keep your true purpose top of mind .

Check out these examples from our main characters.

JESSICA

Jessica loves to-do lists. They keep her busy life on track, but she isn't finding success using this same strategy with her financial goals. She creates lists of what she'd like to accomplish financially, but it quickly turns to overwhelm. The overwhelm then turns to doubt, and she pushes it all to the back burner for a few months until she begins to think about planning her finances again. She wants out of the cycle. Jessica loves the idea of tackling her financial goals step by step; this simplifies the process for her, and immediately, a weight lifts off her shoulders.

Here are the goals Jessica came up with, separated into buckets based on their time frames:

0 to 2 years: I Got Love for You Bucket

I want to go on a big vacation every year. I've been having fun going on yoga retreats in exotic places, and I'd like to go on one each year.

2 to 5 years: Big Things Are Coming Bucket

I want to be able to pay for a wedding if I meet the right guy. I'll definitely need a new car within the next 5 years. I've had my current car for so long; I definitely deserve an upgrade.

5 to 10 years: Home Sweet Home Bucket

I'd love to be in a position within the next 10 years where I could put a down payment on a home.

More than 10 years: Rockin' Retirement Bucket

I want to make sure I'm saving enough for retirement. I am doing the match my company offers right now in my 401(k), but how do I know if that's enough?

ASHLEY

Ashley feels stuck goal planning. She is happy, but something feels off. She thinks about where she wants to be 5 years from now. What does her personal life look like? Where is she living? What is she doing? Who is she with? What does her professional life look like? Is she doing a similar job? Is she with the same company?

A light bulb goes off for Ashley. She realizes even though she's happy at work, she wants to have more creative control over the product launches. Her ideal job is to be an interior designer for high-end homes. She already does this for fun within her network of friends and family. This process gives her creative control, and she loves seeing her ideas come to life.

Keep in mind, Ashley runs through an entire list of reasons why she couldn't become an entrepreneur. She quickly realizes this is Sulky Suzie talking, and she moves through it. She creates a realistic plan for starting her own interior design business part time. The idea of building her company part time lifts a weight she didn't even know existed. She feels a new purpose and motivation and greater clarity in her goal planning.

Here's what Ashley came up with:

0 to 2 years: Wedding Extras Bucket

I already have five months' worth of expenses saved as an emergency fund and would like to build this up to six months' worth.

I want to be able to cover additional wedding costs if my fiancé and I go over the budget we have mapped out.

2 to 5 years: Future Condo Bucket

We'd like to buy a starter home or condo, if possible, or is that not a good idea? Renting feels like we're giving our money away, but owning a home seems really stressful and restrictive. (Note how Ashley is uncertain about this goal. That's okay. You can always change your mind later, but if you wait until you're completely certain to start planning for your goals, you'll be behind.)

5 to 10 years: Dream Job Bucket

Have a small business and possibly leave my current job? That would be incredible!

More than 10 years: Relaxation Retirement Bucket

I want to save enough to stop working one day. My mom will never be able to retire. She seems tired all the time. I don't want that for my life.

MIKE AND SARAH

Mike and Sarah need to spend a lot of time on goal planning. They like having a mediator because things get heated quickly when they discuss money. They both get defensive because neither wants to give up their priorities for the other. They don't know how to reach a middle ground.

What they decide to do—and what you should try if you're in the same situation—is to first do this exercise individually. They each write out their goals and then rank them in order of importance to them. Then they come together and listen to each other before taking any action.

Having their goals circulating in their minds had caused unnecessary stress. Once they shared their goals on paper, they found common ground. They couldn't believe they didn't do this earlier. This exercise emphasizes the importance of saying hello to the discomfort rather than ignoring it.

Here's what they came up with:

0 to 2 years: Hey Hey Vacay Bucket

We'd like to be able to go on one big trip and a few weekend getaway trips each year. We don't know if this is realistic. Sarah wants to plan for bigger goals in life but doesn't want to be penny pinching all the time. She doesn't want to feel bad about enjoying her life now. She wants to find a happy medium.

2 to 5 years: Mini Me Bucket

We want to start planning for a baby.

5 to 10 years: Bye Bye Debt Bucket

We want to have Sarah's student loans paid off.

We want to sell our home and buy a bigger house for our growing family.

More than 10 years: Future Presidents Bucket

We want to support our children through college and hope to pay for them each to attend a four-year college.

More than 10 years: Retirement in Style Bucket

We know we need to save for retirement. We don't know if we're doing enough right now. It's far away and easy not to think about.

THE THREE WHY TEST

As you think about your goals, I want to challenge you to the Three Why Test. Once you come up with a want or goal, ask yourself why it is important to you. Then whatever your answer is, ask yourself why again. Then repeat one final time. This exercise is great because it helps you understand your true motivator.

Here's an example:

My more-than-10-year goal:

Be able to pay for my kids to attend a four-year college.

First Why: Why do I want to pay for my kids' college tuitions?

Because it's important to me that they graduate without student loans.

Second Why: Why is having them graduate without student loans important to me?

I want to give my kids a head start like my parents gave me. My parents sacrificed so much to move to a country that was foreign to them. They had to learn an entirely new language (English is my mother's and father's third language) and leave their families to move to the United States to raise a family together.

Third Why: Why is my parents' sacrifice important to my kids' college tuition?

My parents always put me first. Looking back, they had no time for themselves. They never threw that in my face. I want to honor them by showing them their struggle and efforts live on. As a result of their commitments, they created the groundwork for a new generation of Americans to be well educated and have a life full of opportunity in the land of the free.

Wow. That gives me chills and gets me choked up. That's a powerful reason why I want to pay for my kids to go to college. Understanding my why inspires me. I get excited about saving for their college because it's not about money. Money is the source, not the outcome. To me, this outcome can't be described in words.

> **Empowered Planning Golden Rule:** The side effect of working toward goals you set for yourself is pride.

It's easy to sit back and wish you were born into wealth. But setting a goal and doing the work to achieve it builds character, brings joy and pride, and makes you *YOU*. If we're honest with ourselves, the journey is where we feel true fulfillment.

JOURNAL EXERCISE

Now it's your turn! Goal planning will be what you make of it. If you put little effort into it, that's what you'll get out. I say go big. Figure out what you want out of life altogether.

Keep in mind, it's totally normal for your goals to change with time. As you work toward a goal, things will pop up, and you may want to pivot. If you need to tweak your plan, then you'll tweak it. I took a one-year break from working after I had my son. I didn't "plan" that. It's okay; life happens.

Right now, we want to keep moving forward. If you get stuck, use something as a placeholder. Do an emotional check-in. If you're not having fun, you're doing it wrong!

Another trick that works is to do this with a friend. Treat it like a conversation about life, and the financial goals will start pouring out. Share with them what exercise you're doing and treat them to coffee or lunch. It'll be fun for them, too, and bring you closer together as friends.

Here are some questions to get you thinking about this from a creative place:

- Close your eyes and really picture yourself 5 years from now. Where are you and what are you doing? What does your professional life look like and what does your personal life look like?
- What kind of lifestyle do you want to have (e.g., annual international vacations, host dinner parties for friends, have a home with a guest suite for the in-laws)?
- What are some things you want to make sure you can do within the next 2 years that require a financial commitment (e.g., vacation to Hawaii, new car)?
- What are your personal/professional goals for 5 years from now? What about 10 years from now? What about more than 10 years from now? The more detail, the better.
- Why, Why, Why—As you come up with your answers, ask and answer why you want that particular goal.

KEY TAKEAWAYS

In this chapter, we talked about how important it is to identify what you truly want from your life and go after it. You need to figure out what financial freedom means to you and create goals that reflect where you want to be.

Remember the Empowered Planning Golden Rule: The side effect of working toward goals you set for yourself is pride.

In creating your goals, separate them into buckets by their time frames:

- 0 to 2 years
- 2 to 5 years
- 5 to 10 years
- More than 10 years

Before we can figure out how to make your goal a reality, we need to know your starting point. In the next chapter, we'll look at where you stand today. This will help you figure out how to get to your end goal. Let's get to it.

CHAPTER 4

KNOWING YOUR NUMBERS

Imagine you're building your dream home. The process starts out with excitement, hope, and inspiration. After the initial euphoria, you get overwhelmed with all the decisions. You are emotionally exhausted. You hire a builder under mental fatigue. You begin to focus on what inspires you to bounce back: the interior details. You spend your time making Pinterest boards for flooring, kitchen countertops, cabinets, the list goes on! You are swept away by the variety of options for paint colors. Fast forward nine months, you're close to the final stages. You can see yourself in your dream home.

Then a month of intense rainstorms hit. Neighborhoods flood with water. As things settle down, your house literally starts to sink. You work with the builder and the city. It turns out, the builder took short cuts. The foundation for the home is faulty. They need to start from scratch. You find out your builder has a poor reputation in your city. You are standing outside your sinking house wondering where the heck you go from here.

Am I being dramatic? Yes, but for good reason. I have created hundreds of financial plans for wealthy families across the country. I've delivered more than 500 live personal finance workshops speaking with thousands of people. I have seen it all. I've seen the results when a strong financial foundation has been laid. I've seen the catastrophic results when the foundation was shaky at best. I will forever preach that without a strong financial foundation, nothing else matters.

Here is some food for thought. Abraham Maslow was an American psychologist who observed the innate curiosity of people. He believed we need to satisfy our basic needs before moving toward other desires. In his paper "A Theory of Human Motivation," he created a hierarchy of needs to help illustrate his findings. The bottom of the pyramid represents basic needs, such as food, water, safety, and security. The middle of the pyramid represents psychological needs, such as meaningful friendships, self-esteem, and accomplishments. The top of the pyramid represents self-fulfilling needs, such as achieving your full potential.

See the illustration:

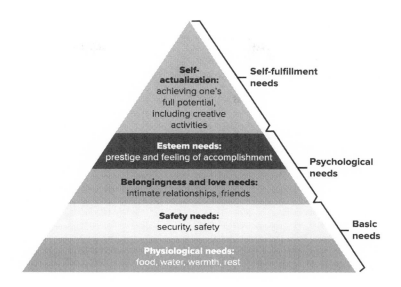

Maslow believed if we don't satisfy our basic and psychological needs, it would be challenging to find the motivation to pursue self-fulfillment. Financial security is a basic need. If you're standing on shaky financial ground, you'll be pulled away from following your passions. A strong financial foundation is the backbone of having options. When you have financial security, you are in control of your money; your money doesn't control you.

Most people want to jump right into investing because it sounds sexy, right? Investing is full of allure. Financial planning, budgeting—those sound like something your mom is into. Yup, I just made fun of your mom. It won't happen again. Before we get to the juicy stuff, we must find clarity. You need to know your numbers. Much of the work you'll do in the following chapters is built off what you do now.

BUDGETING: YUCKY, LIFESTYLE GUIDE: OOH LA LA!

What's the first thing that comes to mind when you hear the word *budget*? I immediately feel like I'm in trouble. I've worked with thousands of people, and it's rare to see a client look comfortable when I bring up budgeting. That's why I want to shift your thinking away from that ugly word. Bye-bye, budgeting—hello, Lifestyle Guide! A Lifestyle Guide is a spending plan that helps you prioritize what you want in life. The numbers serve as a guide to get you where you want to be. This starts with knowing how much you spend. Oh, and don't go shaming yourself for spending money. If Sulky Suzie pops her head out, you know what to do.

CREATING YOUR LIFESTYLE GUIDE

Jot down what you think you spend each month. Don't overthink this. Write down a number you think is accurate. You can use the book margins or grab a Post-it. Then go through your expenses. I recommend you use a guide, worksheet, or app such as mint. com. I created a Lifestyle Guide that is available in the digital assets. You can also look through your bank records and credit card statements from the last three months. Choose whichever option works best for you. The point is to stop winging it. The goal of this exercise is clarity. You want transparency on what you spend.

First, you want to know your MUST HAVE expenses. MUST HAVE expenses are things you can't live without. For example, mortgage or rent, groceries, utilities, cell phones, and so forth. Total these up to see your baseline expenses.

Next, you want to know your NICE TO HAVE expenses. NICE TO HAVE expenses are things such as dining out, your Amazon account, Netflix, and so forth. They're nice to have, but you don't need Netflix to survive. Or do you? I recommend going through an annual calendar for these expenses since they vary from month to month. For example, January: ski trip to Park City, February: Valentine's Day family gifts, April: spring break trip to see the grandparents. You can use an average of what you typically spend each month once you total these up.

Now that you know how much you spend, how accurate was your number before you did the exercise? This is important. You want to understand how in touch you are with your spending. If you're way off, this is an opportunity to become more aware. No judgment; this is a learning experience. They don't teach this stuff in school, which is why most people are winging it.

MONEY MINDSET CHECK-IN

How are you feeling right now?

If you're great, then keep on moving.

If you're feeling overwhelmed or stressed about this topic, sit with it. Set a timer for five minutes. Acknowledge the thought, reframe your thinking, and move through it. Remember that avoidance is negative reinforcement. Growth happens when you move through it. You got this!

INDUSTRY TIPS

I want to shed some light on what the industry has discovered as a recipe for success. Let's take a look at some general rules of thumb for spending. Use these as a guide.

Empowered Planning Golden Rule: No more than 50% of your take-home pay (after taxes) should go toward your MUST HAVE expenses.

Empowered Planning Golden Rule: No more than 28% of your gross income (before taxes) should go toward your monthly housing payment. This includes your principal, interest, taxes, and insurance.

Just because a bank approves you for a mortgage doesn't mean you can comfortably afford the payment each month. Keep in mind, the higher your monthly housing payment is, the less you can put toward achieving your other financial goals. That's why these rules exist.

Empowered Planning Golden Rule: No more than 30% of your take-home pay should go toward your NICE TO HAVE expenses.

We can get caught paying for things out of convenience. When you become more aware of your spending, you can intentionally spend money, aka save money, toward goals that really matter to you. Becoming more aware of your spending habits allows you to put intention toward what really matter to you.

In theory, with no more than 50% going to MUST HAVE expenses and no more than 30% going to NICE TO HAVE expenses, this leaves at least 20% available to go toward your savings goals. Having these rules as guidelines can be helpful so you're not simply winging it. As you implement saving and investing strategies, you can iron out your specifics. You will get very clear on what works for you now.

Empowered Planning Golden Rule: You should have an emergency fund of three to six months of your monthly expenses.

The standard is to use three months when you live in a two-income household. Use six months when you live in a one-income household OR you both work for the same company. I also suggest you err on the side of six months if you are more established in your career. Replacing higher income can be challenging, especially in sluggish economic times. You want to give yourself flexibility. An emergency fund is a must. Create a line item in your Lifestyle Guide to establish your emergency fund if you don't already have one.

> **Empowered Planning Golden Rule:** Automate your saving as much as possible.

Saving is easier when you don't have to think about it all the time. Automatically saving and investing a portion of your income ensures you're saving regularly, and then whatever is left, you can spend without the guilt. I'll talk about automating more in Chapter 11.

DEALING WITH VARIABLE INCOME

It can be challenging to stick with spending guidelines when your pay varies from month to month. This can cause a feeling of not being in control of your finances. I recommend you use two accounts to establish consistency. Here is the breakdown:

Account 1 is your getting-paid account. You deposit all your earnings in here.

Account 2 is your paycheck account. Create a biweekly or monthly automatic transfer into this account to cover your expenses. Here's an example:

> Your total expenses are $6,000 per month, which include your savings goals.

> You get paid $10,000 in commissions this month.

The $10,000 gets directly deposited into Account 1, your getting-paid account.

Every two weeks, $3,000 is automatically transferred into Account 2, your paycheck account. Each month, you receive a total of $6,000 in Account 2, your paycheck account, to cover all your expenses.

The extra $4,000 in Account 1, your getting-paid account, will stay in there.

Over time, you are building a reserve in Account 1. That way, if you have a slow month, you have money to pull from without creating stress. This may take some time. Run the numbers to figure out a realistic time frame for when this will be set on auto-pilot. Then have patience. You got this!

JOURNAL EXERCISE

As you look through your Lifestyle Guide, how accurate was your initial number compared to your actual spending total?

Were you surprised by any areas of your spending? For example, I'm always surprised at how much I spend on dining out.

Where would you like to make some changes?

Are there any areas you are willing to cut back on? For example, are you actively using all the streaming services you pay for each month?

What are the things you aren't willing to cut back on? My husband is an avid road cyclist. Although his cycling expenses fall into our NICE TO HAVE category, it's not an expense that's negotiable for him. Make a list of your own nonnegotiables. Don't start cutting out everything you enjoy. What's the point of that?

LIFESTYLE GUIDES IN ACTION

Let's look at our main characters to see some Lifestyle Guides in action.

JESSICA

Jessica's mindset is that since nothing is wrong financially in her life, she doesn't need to have a budget. She has enough money each month to pay her bills, go out with her friends, and still save. Tracking her spending is not a priority. When Jessica sat down to create her Lifestyle Guide, she procrastinated on more than one occasion. Turns out, Drama Queen Jolene was on the scene. Jessica experienced high anxiety each time she sat down to look at her expenses. Avoiding this exercise brought immediate relief.

What's the solution? Acknowledge the thought, reframe your thinking, and move through it. Jessica recruited a close friend to create Lifestyle Guides together. Jessica liked the idea of making this a social and friendly challenge. She and her girlfriend had been talking about getting to the next level with their finances, which made the timing perfect. They picked a Saturday, worked on it as much as they could, and went out for dinner and drinks afterward. Once it was said and done, Jessica was happily surprised because her situation wasn't bad at all. She had this aha moment. For Jessica, the thought of the unknown caused more anxiety than the reality.

Jessica finds the spending guidelines helpful. She didn't know how to measure this in the past. Raising her awareness around where her money was going helped her spend with intention. Because Jessica was a free spender, it was important she look over the last six months of her credit card statements for accuracy. Each month was different. She realized she was overspending on gifts for family and friends. Jessica enjoys giving thoughtful gifts. She is still able to do this inexpensively.

ASHLEY

Ashley had a good grip on her spending. This became a habit in her early 20s. She saw her mom struggling and prioritized saving. When she sat down to create her Lifestyle Guide, she was completely in touch with what she was spending on a monthly basis.

The exercise brought Ashley's attention to her MUST HAVE expenses. She spends 60% of her take-home pay on her MUST HAVEs. Being over the Empowered Planning Golden Rule by 10% was eating away at her. She was disappointed. Previous to this exercise, she thought she was doing great on her spending levels. She then spiraled into thinking she won't be able to meet her financial goals.

Knock, knock. Guess who? Sulky Suzie is at the door. You know the drill: acknowledge the thought, reframe your thinking, and move through it.

Ashley's biggest MUST HAVE expense was her rent. Since her lease was month to month, it was a great time to explore real estate options, and she found a place with cheaper rent. By the end of all of this, Ashley had the reassurance that working on her finances was what she needed. She was winging it, and this exercise helped her navigate the wacky world of finance.

MIKE AND SARAH

Mike and Sarah each dug into their bank account statements, credit card statements, and individual expenses before bringing it all together. Since they're still overcoming their fear of talking about finances together, they went through that three-step process of acknowledge the thought, reframe the thinking, and move through it. As part of their solution, they hosted dinner that night with two other couples as their reward for doing this exercise.

Sarah was out of touch with her spending. Her actual numbers were completely off. She was really surprised by her spending. She was ready to start making changes if she had a plan or direction. She didn't want to feel restricted or like she was on a budget. Creating a Lifestyle Guide that would help them reach their financial goals felt exciting. Most of their overspending came from entertainment and dining out. They didn't need to cut it out completely, but they could dial it back. A light bulb went off for Sarah. She was at a crossroads. She could continue living for today only or start planning for the life she really wanted with Mike. Sarah and Mike grew much closer during this exercise. They went from arguing about spending to compromising for each other. It was amazing!

MAKING THE MOST OF YOUR LIFESTYLE GUIDE

This is your Lifestyle Guide. You're in control. If you find places you want to cut back, that's great. If you're happy with your spending as is, great. Your spending should align with the lifestyle you want.

Having routine check-ins is helpful. I recommend going through your Lifestyle Guide once every quarter. Pick a reward for yourself after you're done with the exercise, such as going on a hike, to the beach, to a nice restaurant, or on a date night. Choose something you'll look forward to. If you're planning with a partner, do an emotional check-in. My husband and I still get stiff and defensive when we do this. I don't want to feel guilty about a latte and avocado toast. He doesn't want to feel guilty about his bike maintenance or gear. By planning something fun for us to do later that day, we confirm our commitment to each other. Planning your finances becomes intimate in an endearing way.

If you were way off on your estimated expenses versus your actual expenses, revisit your Lifestyle Guide every month. I do this from time to time when things feel like they're out of whack. If I wait three months to do this, I'm not able to make impactful change. Once I'm in a rhythm, I go back to quarterly check-ins. Figure out what method brings results for you.

Avoid becoming obsessed with your Lifestyle Guide. Every now and then, I come across someone who is so stuck on creating a perfect Lifestyle Guide that they're not able to move forward through the planning process. Knock, knock. Guess who? Yup, that's right. It's Drama Queen Jolene. And she's in a mood. This feeling of "I need to get this right before I can move on" is fear of making a mistake. Your Lifestyle Guide is forever changing. It should be fluid to match real life. Beating yourself up for spending more than you wanted or not having a "perfect" Lifestyle Guide is a losing battle.

Knowing what you spend and adjusting along the way is the tip of the iceberg. The purpose is to help you live the life you want today while creating a plan to reach your financial goals tomorrow. If you get hung up on your spending, you're missing the whole point. I say that in the nicest way possible.

KEY TAKEAWAYS

Walking on shaky financial ground will pull you away from following your passions in life. To build a strong foundation, you need to know what you're starting with by going through a budgeting exercise. Having clarity on what you spend each month will help you reach your financial goals.

To know your numbers, use a worksheet, my Lifestyle Guide, or an app. Do the work without judgment. You are raising awareness to bring changes if needed. Do an emotional check-in. If you feel resistance, acknowledge the thought, reframe your thinking, and move through it.

It's up to you how to use your Lifestyle Guide, but here are some helpful industry tips:

- **Empowered Planning Golden Rule:** No more than 50% of your take-home pay (after taxes) should go toward your MUST HAVE expenses.
- **Empowered Planning Golden Rule:** No more than 28% of your gross income (before taxes) should go toward your monthly housing payment. This includes your principal, interest, taxes, and insurance.
- **Empowered Planning Golden Rule:** No more than 30% of your take-home pay should go toward your NICE TO HAVE expenses.
- **Empowered Planning Golden Rule:** You should have an emergency fund of three to six months of your monthly expenses.
- **Empowered Planning Golden Rule:** Automate your saving as much as possible.

Your Lifestyle Guide is a guide for you to take your finances to the next level. Your life is always changing; your Lifestyle Guide should mimic that. Even though this can get uncomfortable, you're doing it. That's what growth feels like. You got this!

Now that you have a basic idea of where you stand in terms of income and expenses, in the next chapter, we'll look at how to master your debt and credit.

CHAPTER 5

MASTERING YOUR DEBT AND CREDIT

Picture this: You've been busting your butt at work putting in long hours. You are beyond ready for a vacation. You talk to some friends, and you finally all agree on a resort in Maui to take a final hoorah vacay! Some of your friends have kids; others are planning that adventure soon. It's not realistic you could do this again as a couples-only getaway. You all say yes. Even though you're able to book your flight on points, you are still having to pony up $5,000 for the trip. You've been saving for a new home and don't want to touch that money. You always pay off your credit card each month, so you'll make an exception. This one time. The $100 a month minimum payment seems reasonable, and it's way better than having to dip into your savings to come up with the $5,000. You convince yourself this is a good decision.

Guess how much interest you'll pay in total for this $5,000 vacation? Guess how many years it'll take you to pay off this vacation by making monthly payments of $100? You credit card company charges you 20% interest, which leaves you paying a whopping $10,000 when all is said and done. Oh, and it takes you over 9 years to pay it off! Wowza. Most people inherently know that carrying credit card debt isn't "good," but when you see the numbers broken down that like, it's really eye opening. Hopefully, this serves as a motivator to approach debt in the right way.

Let me keep it real right now. Debt isn't the boogie man. I want to teach you the difference between good debt and bad debt. We all have debt, it's totally normal, and we are not bad, shameful people. The key to debt is managing it through organization, prioritization, and automation. If you start to play the shame game around your debt, just remember that's Sulky Suzie and Drama Queen Jolene. Acknowledge how you feel, reframe your thinking, and move through it. You got this!

GOOD DEBT VERSUS BAD DEBT

Debt is classified as "good" when it's used to purchase things that grow in value and increase your earning power. In contrast, bad debt is borrowing money for things that decrease in value. Typically, good debt is associated with low interest rates, and bad debt is usually associated with higher interest rates.

Let's go through some examples.

MORTGAGES

Mortgages are good debt. You can build equity, and in general, interest rates on mortgages are reasonable in terms of the current interest rate environment. Plus, initial bank fees on your loan, ongoing mortgage interest, and property taxes are all great tax deductions at the end of the year.

BUT there are a ton of other costs associated with owning a home, like home maintenance, repairs, and so on. Rather than having a landlord come in and fix them, you're shelling out the money yourself. It can quickly add up to thousands of dollars. So it's something to be aware of and plan for.

Also keep in mind the Empowered Planning Golden Rule from the last chapter: your total monthly housing payment shouldn't be more than 28% of your gross income, including your principal, interest, taxes, insurance, and any homeowners association fees that apply. A bank might approve you for a higher loan amount, but the larger your mortgage payment, the less flexibility you'll have toward other financial goals.

CREDIT CARDS

Credit cards are an example of bad debt. My friend Jen had bad credit card debt because she assumed everybody did. She was paying more than the minimums each month but not by much, and she was getting charged over 20% interest on her remaining balances. She thought this debt was something that would always be there and wasn't that big of a deal. I showed her how much money was going toward her balances versus how much was going toward interest. This immediately motivated her to start paying her credit cards off. Remember the example from the beginning of the chapter, too—over 9 years and $10,000 to pay off a $5,000 vacay! Yikes.

This isn't to say you shouldn't use credit cards at all, but you should strive to pay off your cards in full as frequently as you can. Also keep in mind that store credit cards tend to have higher interest rates than regular credit cards.

AUTO LOANS

In general, auto loans are bad debt. Why? Most cars lose value over time, and auto loan interest rates tend to have a wide range, sometimes falling on the high side.

Even though it's considered bad debt, you don't need to walk everywhere. You can be smart about how you finance a car. If you are purchasing a car, get quotes from the car dealer and your local bank or credit union.

We're in a unique time with auto loans. The costs of new cars are increasing faster per year than ever before. Technology advancements and new safety features are driving up the prices. Incomes are not rising at the same level, creating an imbalance we haven't seen in the past. Longer financing terms, more than 5 years, are becoming the new norm. This can be problematic because over time, you may owe more than what the car is worth. The longer the loan, the higher the interest rate. A shorter loan will have more-favorable terms. If the car payment is too high, buy a less expensive car. Be mindful of how much you want to spend on a car and what you're giving up in exchange.

FINANCING OF CONSUMER ITEMS

It's typical to apply for financing for bigger purchases, such as a home or car. Financial technology, aka fintech, companies have further expanded the small-debt market. They offer creative financing solutions that we haven't seen before, offering on-the-spot financing for consumer purchases. These tend to be bad debt.

For example, let's say you're purchasing an espresso maker you've been eyeing for months. You get to the checkout page, and you can either pay $899 today or $30 per month. Want that Apple watch? What do you think of 0% for the first sixty days, then equal payments of $50 per month? Next thing you know, you have ten extra payments per month.

It's easy to fall into this trap—even I've done it. I like to pay my credit cards off each month, but it can get tricky around the holiday season with so many gift purchases. For this reason, I opted to select this new, easy financing option for a few items I was purchasing. By the third time I did it, a light bulb went off, and I caught myself in the middle of it all. I realized I wasn't even present to what I was doing. I was acting like a robot. This is merely a nudge to stay in tune with how you're paying for things. Make sure it aligns with what story you want to be writing today. Be aware of these shiny offers, evaluate, and then make a decision.

DEBT PAYOFF JOURNEY

I've mentioned this already, but it's totally normal to have debt. There should be no shame in your debt game. Well, as long as you have a clearly laid-out debt repayment plan. I'll share with you how to organize, prioritize, and automate your debt repayment so you have a plan and are intentionally paying down your debt.

It's easy to get carried away when tackling your debt. You have it in your mind that you want to get rid of it. You become laser focused, trying to throw any and all of your extra money at it. Pace yourself. You want to leave cushion room for you to save toward other goals. For example, if you're throwing all your extra money at your debts, how are you saving for vacations or retirement? It's a balancing act. As you begin to create your Empower Plan, you'll be able to prioritize all your financial goals, not just one. You don't want to get burned out.

For example, let's say you have a thirty-year mortgage at a 4% rate of interest, an auto loan at a 3.5% rate of interest, and a credit card you pay off each month. Your debt repayment plan can be to make one extra payment on your mortgage or auto loan once a year. Or maybe it's to do nothing extra. In this case, it's okay to be okay paying the interest because it's reasonably low and you're using your extra savings to invest in the stock market. The important thing is to consider your options and commit to a plan.

ORGANIZE

As you embark on your payoff journey, simply focus on one task at a time. It's easy to get overwhelmed if you look at everything all at once. Give yourself a break. Take it step by step. The first thing you need to do is get organized. You're not taking any action yet. Gather all the information. I offer a Debt Worksheet in the digital assets that can help you organize everything.

Here are some simple steps to organizing your debt. Answer these questions for each debt you have:

- Who is your loan provider/servicer?
  - Essentially, you want to know who is holding your loan. This may be different from whom you purchased the loan from originally. The loan servicer will be the name of the company on your statement. It's also nice to add them to your list of contacts so you have their customer service information handy.
- What is the principal balance?
  - This is the dollar amount you have outstanding or left to pay on the specific loan.
- What is the interest rate percentage?
- What is your minimum monthly payment?
- What is your projected payoff date?

- If you continue to make the minimum monthly payment, how long will it take you to pay off that specific loan? If you can't clearly see this on your statement, you can request this information from the loan provider/servicer.

Okay. Once you have all your debt organized, you can create a plan of attack. If seeing all your debt in one place stresses you out and your heart rate starts to rise and anxiety creeps in, take that as a sign you're doing it right. I know that sounds counterintuitive, but it's true. Remember when we talked about the consequences of avoidance? By sitting with your debt, you are breaking through your fears. Each time you address this, the easier it will become. Give yourself a hug because who really does the pat on the back thing? You got this!

PRIORITIZE

After organizing, it's time to prioritize. Making your monthly minimum payments is your baseline. You need to do this for all your debts. You then want to focus on knocking some of your debt down faster.

> **Empowered Planning Golden Rule:** Prioritize repaying any debts with an interest rate over 8%.

There are two main prioritization strategies: the avalanche method and the snowball method.

The avalanche method suggests you go after the debts with the highest rates of interest first. This makes the most financial sense. By using this method, you will save the most money in interest payments.

The snowball method suggests you go after the debts with the smallest balances first. Although this doesn't make the most financial sense, it helps you build momentum and can keep you motivated. Some people find this the most enticing way to pay down debt.

Let's say you have the following debts:

$10,000 Major Credit Card at 22% interest

$8,000 Home Furniture Store Card at 18% interest

$5,000 Auto Loan at 4% interest

By using the avalanche method, you would use any extra money you've earmarked to paying down debt toward the $10,000 major credit card that's charging you 22% interest. Once that's paid down, you chip away at the next debt that's charging you the highest rate of interest. In this example, it would be the home furniture store card.

By using the snowball method, you would use your extra money to pay down the auto loan first, then the home furniture store card, then the major credit card. Yes, you are paying more interest this way, but if it keeps you motivated, stick with what works.

There's no right or wrong way to do this. What strategy suits your personality best? You can even start with the snowball method to knock down some debts and then switch over to the avalanche method once you have some quick wins in your pocket! Whatever you decide, write it down. Stick to it.

AUTOMATE

After you've established your plan for knocking down debt, automate it. If you have to manually log in and pay off the debt, you might forget and accidentally spend the money you need to pay off the debt on something else. If it's automated, you don't have to worry about it.

Here are the steps for automation:

- Establish online access.
  - You may already be doing this, but if not, jump on board. Establish online account access with each of your debts. You want to have quick and easy access.
- Set up monthly autopayments for your minimums plus a little extra.
- Set up a recurring calendar reminder for every six months to see if you can increase these extra payments toward your loans.

STUDENT LOANS

If you don't have any student loans or already conquered this part of your life, go ahead and skip this section. If you're in the process of paying off student loan debt, then please allow me to be your cheerleader. Student loan debt can come with a mixed bag of emotions. Let's start with what I believe is the most important. Take a moment to reflect on the valuable friendships and relationships you formed while pursuing your degree. Now think about opportunities that presented themselves to you because of your qualifications after earning your degree. Although carrying student loan debt can be burdensome, don't forget all the experiences that came with it both directly and indirectly.

Let me share a story. My friend Karen earned a bachelor's degree in psychology and immediately went on to get her master's degree. After several years working in the field, she wasn't sure if this is what she really wanted to do. She felt handcuffed to her degree because she still had a ton of student loan debt. She was unsure of how to transition into another industry. She began to explore other ways she could use her degree and, at a networking event, met her husband. I realize hearing this story can sound cheesy, but that meeting changed her life for the better. While she was falling in love, space opened up in her workplace for a new opportunity. She started to oversee a new curriculum. She started to get a lot of satisfaction from her work and found a way to balance her career and personal life.

This is a creative way of looking at your debt, but there's evidence all around you of this trickle-down effect. Focus on the positives when you start to get discouraged because you are not your debt. It is part of your journey right now, but it is not *WHO* you are. You are layers and layers of a beautiful person. Remember that always.

Student loans are considered good debt because they're an investment in your career and increase your earning potential. In general, rates on government loans are lower than private loans. A common question I get is, "What's the difference between a subsidized and unsubsidized loan?" A subsidized loan does not accrue or build interest while you're earning your degree. These interest payments are paid for, or subsidized, by the federal government. An unsubsidized loan starts accruing or building interest as soon as the loan is paid to the school. You are not required to make payments until six months after graduating school, but your loans are building interest on top of the initial amount you borrowed.

Paying off your student loans is a very similar process to what you should do with any other existing debt. Focus on one task at a time: organize, prioritize, and automate. You can use the specific Student Loan Debt Worksheet I provide in the digital assets.

As with other debts, making your monthly minimum payments is your baseline. You need to do this, and there's really not any wiggle room. There are exceptions if you're in a financial bind, and if that happens, you can explore possible deferment or forbearance. I encourage you to pay your student loan debt off faster if possible. Factor the extra payments into your Lifestyle Guide so it becomes a part of your process and overall thinking.

There are a couple of other options to keep in mind with student loans, including consolidation or refinancing and employer-sponsored student loan repayment programs.

CONSOLIDATING AND REFINANCING OPTIONS

Explore consolidation and refinance options. These are two separate things, and you need to do equal amounts of homework into both before you make any decisions.

Student loan consolidation is a process where you take out a new loan. This new loan is used to pay off your other existing student loans. Rather than having multiple loans with unique interest rates and monthly payments, you have only one.

Student loan refinancing is a process where your lender reworks the terms of your existing student loan debt. Your lender pays off your existing loans with a new one at a lower interest rate.

If your loan servicer or bank does offer any consolidation or refinance options, make sure you understand the terms. A good test to see if you understand the terms of the offer is to clearly explain it to a friend. If you get tripped up or your friend has questions you can't answer, go back to the loan servicer and ask questions until you feel comfortable enough to make a decision.

Weigh the pros and cons before making a final decision. Although consolidation or refinance may come with an over-all lower monthly payment, it may extend the length of your repayment period. This could cause you to make extra interest payments in the long run. You also may lose benefits that come with the loans you currently have. For example, if you're receiving any loan cancellation benefits from your employer, you may lose these benefits by consolidating or refinancing. When in doubt, just ask and make sure you understand it all before doing anything.

EMPLOYER-SPONSORED STUDENT LOAN REPAYMENT PROGRAMS

Some employers offer student loan repayment programs to attract and retain talented employees to their firms. These programs are similar to how a retirement savings plan, such as a 401(k), works. Your employer will contribute a fixed amount—for example, $50 to $100 per month. As long as you make your payments on time, your employer will continue to give you this benefit. Companies can choose different benefits and the terms by which they are paid.

If you have student loans, bring this up to your employer and see if they've been looking into adopting this policy. From research available, it seems many companies are looking to adopt these plans. It doesn't hurt to ask. If you're looking for new employment, it's something to keep in mind and ask about in interviews.

MASTERING YOUR CREDIT

Having great credit—as proven through your credit score—is something you can and should master. Your credit score should never catch you off guard. It should make your life easier, not complicate it. By understanding a few key things, you can master your credit and not have to worry about it for the rest of your life.

WHY DOES HAVING GOOD CREDIT MATTER?

We'll start with the obvious reason good credit matters: the better your credit score, the better the interest rate and terms you'll receive when financing anything you buy, such as a house or a car. There are several other less obvious but important reasons to have good credit:

- Employment—You know when you get to the happy stage of the interview process and you get offered the job? Then they ask you to sign all this stuff so they can dig into your personal life? Many employers check your credit before they officially hire you. They want to see if you are financially responsible. Depending on the results, they could hesitate to hire you.
- Business Loans—Do you want to start a business? Or expand your existing business? You may consider taking out a loan to get you going. You'll need good credit to get started.
- Day-to-Day Living—That is, rental agreements and utility services, such as gas, electric, and water. Just about every landlord runs a credit check before renting to someone. If you have poor credit, you could miss out on the apartment of your dreams. Additionally, when you want to turn on your utilities, even your cell phone, you are borrowing the service for one month before you pay the bill. Many utility companies will pull your credit score before providing you services. They use this to predict how you will treat your future obligations to them.

WHAT MAKES UP YOUR CREDIT SCORE?

Your credit score is monitored by three main credit bureaus: Transunion, Equifax, and Experian. These credit bureaus keep track of your debt characteristics and give you a score. Typically, when you apply for financing, the bank will take the lowest of the three scores. I like to compare how the credit bureaus determine your credit score to my childhood next-door neighbor, Nancy. She was, how can I say this nicely, moody. If she just had her grandkids over, she'd be outside waving. The next day, if you went in her yard to retrieve your Skip-It that got away, she would come outside and scream, "Get off my property!" This is how the credit bureaus can seem, like ol' Nancy. One day, your credit score is doing great, but then it takes a hit and dips many points. Once you understand how the credit bureaus work, you can play their game. Let's bust all those credit myths and see what truly makes up your score.

Your payment history makes up 35% of your score. Do you pay your bills on time, are they made late, have you missed any, do you have any bills in collections? The more recently that you've missed a payment or gone late, the bigger impact it has on your credit score. It's important to understand that the minimum amounts due will affect how much your credit score declines. Going late on a larger payment, such as a mortgage, can have a bigger impact on your credit score. (This is assuming your mortgage balance is much larger than your credit card balance.)

Your credit utilization makes up 30% of your score. The credit bureaus are looking at how much revolving credit you are using versus what you have available. Revolving credit is a credit account that you can repeatedly borrow money from up to a certain limit. The most common types of revolving credit are a credit card and a bank line of credit. You want your ongoing balances to be less than 50% of your available credit limit. Let's look at the balances on Jessica's and Ashley's credit cards as an example.

Jessica has a credit card balance of $4,000, and her credit card limit is $7,000. This makes her available credit $3,000, using 57% of her available credit.

Ashley has a credit card balance of $5,000, and her credit card limit is $13,000. This makes her available credit $7,000, using 38% of her available credit.

Jessica has a rolling balance of $4,000 on her credit card, and Ashley has a rolling balance of $5,000 on her credit card. At first glance, it's easy to assume Jessica has better credit than Ashley. Common sense says that Jessica has less debt than Ashley, but that's not what the credit bureaus care about. Ashley has more credit available to her, and her balance is less than 50% of the credit available. The credit bureaus start to freak out about Jessica's situation. She is getting close to her limit, so she must be in a tight financial spot. If she loses her job, she doesn't have much credit available. They take it upon themselves to alert every possible financial institution by lowering her score each month. The credit bureaus don't look at your bank statements or your pay stubs. All they can see is what's on the credit reports, and they judge you all the time!

The length of your credit history makes up 15% of your score. What is your credit age, how long have you had a history with the credit bureaus? This is straightforward. The longer your credit history, the higher your score. This is assuming you are making your payments on time.

Your credit mix makes up 10% of your credit score. Your credit mix considers your ability to handle different types of credit, such as revolving credit and installment loans. Revolving credit has variable payments each month depending on your overall balance—think credit card. Installment loans have fixed payments for a fixed period of time, such as student loans or a mortgage. Having different types of debt actually increases your credit score!

Credit inquiries make up 10% of your score. If you apply for credit at multiple places in a short period of time, your credit score may decrease. Keep in mind, applying for a job that runs a credit check or setting up utilities doesn't count as an inquiry. You have to specifically apply for credit. The credit bureaus have no idea what's going on in your financial life. If they see you're applying for a credit card with a furniture company and applying for a mortgage, they're freaking out. Home lenders will tell you not to have your credit run during the home loan process. You should be able to shop lenders within the same industry without affecting your score, but this isn't guaranteed.

MONITORING YOUR CREDIT

You should monitor your credit on a regular basis and keep track of what the credit bureaus are reporting. Don't wait until you find the home of your dreams to discover an old collection from your college years. You can often add credit monitoring as a service from your credit card company or bank; it's a great place to start! With fraud rampant these days, you also want to see if anyone has opened any credit in your name. It's important to monitor who's accessing your credit.

You can also take advantage of the free full credit report you get from each of the major rating agencies, Equifax, Transunion, and Experian, once per year. Rather than run all three free credit reports in January, spread them out. Run a free one through Equifax in January, then through Transunion in May, then Experian in September. You can check out CreditKarma.com or Credit.com to get your report. You want to be very cautious of where you are inputting your Social Security number, so triple check it's a reliable source.

You can always sign up for fraud prevention, notification, or a credit freeze. If you freeze your credit, your credit cannot be run unless you unfreeze it. It's a bit inconvenient to have to do a temporary unfreeze, but you know your credit is protected!

TOTAL NET WORTH

Knowing your total net worth gives you a great snapshot of where you stand today financially. Your total net worth is all your assets minus your debts and liabilities. You don't necessarily need to do anything with this number, but it's good to know. You can use the Net Worth Worksheet available in the digital assets to calculate this. I would check your total net worth twice a year. Over time, you want to grow your assets and decrease your debts and liabilities. Don't get discouraged if you're not where you want to be yet. You are a work in progress. You got this!

KEY TAKEAWAYS

Having debt is completely normal. Having debt is part of your journey, but debt is not *who* you are.

Organize, prioritize, and automate your debt repayment strategy so you know what you're working toward and are intentional in getting there. An Empowered Planning Golden Rule is to prioritize paying down debts with interest rates over 8%.

Pace yourself when paying off debt. You should be motivated to pay off your debt but not handcuffed to it. Only you know what the right balance is, but you need to honor this.

There are five factors that make up your credit score: payment history, credit utilization, length of credit history, credit mix, and credit inquiries. Be aware of these and monitor your credit periodically so there aren't any surprises. This way, you'll be in complete control of your credit score.

Understand your total net worth and create a plan to look at this every six months.

Now that you have a strong financial foundation, you can begin putting up the metaphorical walls of your financial house, building higher. In Phase 2 of your Empower Plan, you'll learn the investing essentials and strategies you need to begin working toward all your financial goals.

Phase 2

Learn the Investing Essentials and Explore Strategies

During this phase, you will:

- Learn the investing essentials every investor should know.
- Learn how to invest like the pros.
- Choose an investment strategy that is tailored to your personality.
- Discover the changes in the retirement landscape and how they apply to you now.

CHAPTER 6

GRASPING THE INVESTING ESSENTIALS

Did you know that the number one financial regret women have is not investing more? This is according to a 2018 study published by Merrill and Age Wave. Some women are convinced they need more money to get started. Other women simply don't know where to start.

This needs to change because investing in the stock market is crucial to your financial success. You need to leverage your money. Make it work *for* you. This is your superpower. Even though saving and investing are typically used in conjunction with each other, their functions are very different. Saving money for a goal is the act of taking money from one source, such as your checking account, and putting it aside for future financial use. Investing is the act of participating in the stock market and taking risk for potential reward. It's common for people I take through Empowered Academy to be saving money but not investing. This is where I get excited. You have a superpower, and you're not using it yet. I get to help you bring that to life. Woo-hoo! Watch out world!

I want to get you in the game. I'll teach you how to start using your superpower. First, rather than try to convince you investing is your superpower, let me show you the power of investing.

Let's look at two different scenarios. In each, assume your starting balance is $100 and you have a 7% annual growth rate.

Scenario A

At age 30, you invest $5,000 per year for 10 years. After 10 years, you stop making contributions, making your total contributions $50,000. You keep this money invested, and at age 50, your balance is about $145,800.

Now let's say you want to wait to start investing until you have more money to contribute.

Scenario B

At age 40, you invest $10,000 per year for 10 years. After 10 years, you stop making contributions, which makes your total contributions $100,000. At age 50, your balance is about $148,000.

In Scenario B, you're contributing twice as much as in Scenario A: $100,000 versus $50,000. Even after trying to play catch-up by doubling down on your investment, you have only $2,200 more by age 50. By starting to invest earlier, at age 30, you're able to take advantage of time and compounding interest, which lets you make about the same total money by age 50 even though you're investing less. You end up saving $50,000 by starting early. Think of what else you can do with $50,000.

The moral of this story: You don't need more money to start investing. You simply need to start.

Investing is your superpower. Superpowers are meant to be nurtured. We tend to focus on what we have going on right now, making it natural to push financial goals to the back burner. A common thing I hear is, "Yes, I'd love to start investing, but I have a ton going on right now," or, "I'll do it when I have more money." The truth is, you'll always have things going on because you are a doer. You make things happen. You're rarely going to catch yourself in a position where you're not juggling a lot of balls in the air. Time, more than money, is the most valuable asset you have when investing. Move from confusion to clarity and start using your superpower.

We'll spend the bulk of this chapter diving into the fundamentals of investing. You'll soon be thinking like a savvy investor. I know investing can be overwhelming, but you don't need to know everything. If you simply understand the moving parts, you'll approach investment opportunities with confidence, and you'll be able to assess true investment risk versus anxiety or fear of the unknown. You'll build on your knowledge as time goes on. You got this, girl!

Grab your favorite cup of coffee, a latte, or green tea. It's time to cozy up next to some investing terms and concepts. You're becoming financially fluent, but it doesn't happen overnight. So get comfortable.

WHY YOU SHOULD INVEST YOUR MONEY

Before we dive into all the investment options you have, it's important to understand why you should invest in the first place. Understanding the why can be a great catalyst for taking action, which is our theme. Information is great, but taking action is what will change your life.

GROW YOUR MONEY, CHA-CHING!

Let's start with the obvious reason: you invest to grow your money. Seems pretty straightforward, right? You want to make money. And then you want to make money on your money. Don't be shy about it, we all want more money. It doesn't make you a bad person. You need money to reach your goals, support the lifestyle you want, and support others. Wanting more money just makes you smart, not greedy. There's a *HUGE* difference.

The sooner you start growing your money, the better. I'll give you the money-talk version and then a real-talk example to tie it together.

Here's the money talk: The time value of money is the idea money in your pocket today is more valuable than that same amount of money in your pocket in the future. The main reason is compounding interest. Compounding interest is the money you earn on your initial deposit plus the interest that money earns.

Real talk: Let's say you invest $1,000 today. You earn interest in the amount of $100. Now you have $1,100 that will earn interest. You start making money on the money that you made, which is the extra $100 in this example. This is where people come up with headlines like "Grow your money while you're sleeping." It's compounding interest.

How cool is it that you can make money without having to clock in at your job and put in your eight hours? Get excited about using your superpower. I want you to be so pumped about this that you blow off your *Friends* marathon weekend with the girls. You know, the one where you eat an offensive amount of ice cream. I want you to happily nerd out on the chapters of this book.

KEEPING UP WITH RISING COSTS

You should also invest your money in order to outpace the rising costs of things you'll need in the future. Remember how I said the money in your pocket today is more valuable than the same amount of money in the future? That's partly due to compounding interest, but it's also due to inflation.

Money talk: Inflation is the increase in prices for goods and services in the economy. As inflation increases, your purchasing power decreases. Your purchasing power is the amount you can buy today based on the value of the dollar.

Real talk: The same things you buy today will be more expensive in the future. Let's say you spend $100 on this amazing night cream. You know, the one where you wake up and haven't aged while sleeping? Ten years from now, the cost of your favorite night cream will be more than the $100 it is today. Which means the $100 you have in your pocket today will be worth less in 10 years. It won't be able to buy you the same night cream you could purchase today.

Inflation is an invisible danger. If you have $100 in your checking account today and don't spend it, it will still show up as $100 in 10 years. You won't feel like you lost any money. It doesn't show up as a line item on your statement as "–$10 for inflation." On the other hand, when you invest your money in the stock market, your statement could show a drop in value. That's clearly laid out, making it scary. On the surface, not investing seems easier, which makes inflation a silent killer.

I like to think about inflation as it relates to my life. If I can't see it on a statement or feel it in my pocket, it's kind of meaningless to me. Here's a personal example to help illustrate this further. Being in finance, there's a lot of reading, calculating, and computer-screen staring that goes on. I love to check out of my brain and reality by going to the movies. Years ago, it cost $5, then $8. Now it's about $16 to $25 to see a movie. And I always get popcorn, even if I don't really want it. It's part of my tradition or, more realistically, my habit. I may change how I go to the movies after COVID-19, but up until now, it's been a typical date night away from the kiddos for me and my hubby. If I continue going to the movies, I can expect the prices to keep going up. So I better make sure my money keeps growing as well.

Brainstorm about this in your life to make it more relatable. Take a minute and think about something you spent money on 5 years ago, still spend money on today, and will most likely spend money on in the future. So how has inflation impacted your life?

KEEP MORE MONEY IN YOUR POCKET

The final reason you should invest is to hang on to more of your money. Simply put, you can pay less taxes.

We work hard for our money. Even after affirmations and manifesting money into your life, *you* are the one who puts in the time and energy to pull it all together. I don't know about you, but if I'm going to give money away, I don't want it to be for taxes. I want to pick a charitable cause I'm passionate about and believe in. With the right investing strategies, you can be more tax efficient or even avoid taxes altogether.

So now you've got an idea of the stakes and all you have to gain by investing. Still comfy with your coffee? Okay, great! Let's move on to *how* to invest.

HOW SHOULD YOU INVEST YOUR MONEY?

The most common question I'm asked is, "What should I invest in?" There's no easy answer. Different investments come with different pros and cons.

Before we start, I know that financial jargon can get confusing, especially when you don't use the language daily. To add more confusion, many of these terms can be used differently. For example, the term *portfolio* can be used to reference all your investments, rather than one specific investment. However, you can also refer to the holdings inside of a mutual fund, which is a specific investment, as a portfolio. Be patient and kind to yourself as we dive into this.

Also, be aware that I'm not going to cover everything under the sun. This book isn't intended to make you an expert in all things investing, but it will help you use a simplified approach to investing so you can reach all your financial goals. I'll be focusing on the essentials every investor must know. There are other investment strategies that will not be covered here, such as investing in real estate, currency, commodities, and precious metals, among others.

The three types of investments I *am* going to cover are stocks, bonds, and cash-like instruments. We call each of these an asset class.

Take a look at the chart below, which illustrates the growth of stocks, bonds, cash, and inflation from 1926 through 2016.

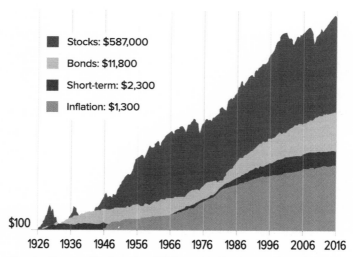

Illustration: Data source: Morningstar, Inc., 2017 (January 1926–December 2016). **Past performance is no guarantee of future results.** The asset class (index) returns reflect the reinvestment of dividends and other earnings. This chart is for illustrative purposes only and does not represent actual or future performance of any investment option. It is not possible to invest directly in a market index. Stocks are represented by the Standard & Poor's 500® Index (S&P 500® Index), bonds by the US Intermediate Government Bond Index, short-term investments by US Treasury bills, and inflation by the Consumer Price Index. Numbers are rounded for simplicity.

I like this chart because it clearly illustrates that over the long haul, stocks outperform bonds and cash and certainly beat inflation. From 1926 through 2016, stocks returned an average 10% annually. Over the same time period, bonds returned an annual average 5.4%, and short-term instruments (aka cash) returned 3.5% per year. Here's how this translates into real life. If you bought something for $100 in 1926, it would run you about $1,300 in 2016. If you invested $100 in bonds in 1926, you'd have $11,800 in 2016, and $100 in short-term instruments purchased in 1926 would get you a mere $2,300 by 2016. If, however, you invested $100 in stocks in 1926, those stocks would be worth $587,000 in 2016. Yes, please! Am I right?

At first glance, stocks look like the best investment. They provide the highest growth over time. Taking a closer look, you see stocks have the most volatility in short-term time frames. This fluctuation in account values comes with heartburn. But seriously, high returns without risk is like a pair of comfortable high heels or unicorns—they don't exist!

There's no magic investment that can bring all upside with no downside. You can't have stability and a ton of growth. Each asset class—meaning stocks, bonds, and cash—has benefits and limitations.

Let's take a deeper look at these asset classes. I'll give you a quick cheat sheet on the role each asset class should play so you can clearly see their advantages and disadvantages.

STOCKS OR EQUITIES

Stocks, or equities, are shares of ownership in a publicly traded company. Stocks come in several forms, but we are going to focus on common shares of stock. These are the most accessible and widely available to purchase. To invest in stocks, you choose stocks that you think will increase in value over time. Stocks have the highest potential return on your investment and can outpace inflation in the long run. Stocks also come with the highest level of risk.

Let's take a look at our cheat sheet:

Do stocks have growth potential?

Yes, stocks have the highest potential return on your investment over time.

Do stocks protect against inflation?

Yes, stocks are your best bet against this silent money killer. Over time, stocks tend to outpace inflation, so you can outpace the rising costs of things you buy.

Do stocks provide stability, aka principal preservation?

No, stocks are volatile and have short-term swings that can cause anxiety.

Do stocks offer liquidity?

It depends. Yes, stocks are liquid (easily turned into cash you can spend) in the sense you can sell them and get your cash within a few days. But no, they are not liquid in that the prices of stocks fluctuate daily. If you need cash quickly, you might have to take a loss on your investment in order to get it. For this reason, stocks shouldn't be used for short-term money goals.

BONDS OR FIXED INCOME

A bond is a loan to a company or government that pays you a fixed rate of return for a set period. Hence the name fixed income.

For example, if Verizon wants to raise capital for a new project, they may issue debt in the form of a bond to the general public. They could offer a ten-year bond that will pay you 5% interest. Let's say you buy $10,000 worth of this particular Verizon bond. You are lending Verizon money for 10 years while they pay you 5% interest ($500) each year. At the end of the 10 years, they return your initial investment amount of $10,000, and you've also earned $5,000 in interest along the way.

Let's take a look at our cheat sheet:

Do bonds have growth potential?

Maybe. This depends on the interest rate environment at the time you are looking to sell your bond and a variety of other factors. (See the example I give in a moment about diamond earrings.) Growth isn't the intention of owning bonds.

Do bonds protect against inflation?

Maybe. This depends on what interest rates are being offered at the time. If a bond has a low interest rate, it may not be able to keep pace with inflation, which has been an average of about 2.5% per year over the last 20 years.

Do bonds provide stability, aka principal preservation?

Yes. That's the whole point. Assuming you hold bonds to the point of maturity, meaning when the bond comes due or expires, they offer a stable investment and pay you a reasonable rate of interest. If you sell them prior to maturity, you may lose money. Bonds should be bought with the intention of holding them until they mature.

Do bonds offer liquidity?

It depends. Yes, bonds are liquid in the sense you can sell them to create cash. But no, bonds aren't liquid because you have to find someone to buy them. You sell them in an open marketplace. Depending on the size of your bonds, the current interest rate environment, and so forth, this could take more than a few days. You also may have to sell them for less than what you paid, depending on a variety of factors.

Think about it like this: Let's say your special someone buys you diamond earnings for your birthday. They're beautiful, sparkly, all the things. After a couple of years, you realize you've worn them only a handful of times and would actually love a necklace instead. You go to sell your diamond earrings, and what you can get depends on the current demand. Are the kinds you have still in style? Have diamond prices gone up? Is the economy booming?

Is everybody getting new shiny digs? Or maybe it's a recession and people aren't spending money on extras these days. It's similar with bonds. You need to shop the marketplace, and depending on a variety of factors, you *may* be able to make money or break even, but you may also lose money. This can get more complex, so I wouldn't recommend buying bonds with the intention of trading them for a profit.

CASH-LIKE INSTRUMENTS

Cash as an investment comes in many different forms. Aside from holding cash in a checking account, you can own it as an investment in various ways, such as an interest-bearing savings accounts, a certificate of deposit (CD), or a money market fund. Savings accounts and CDs may lock you into certain terms since you're earning more interest than you would in a checking account. Ask questions and make sure you understand what you're signing up for.

Let's go to our cheat sheet:

Does cash have growth potential?

No, cash-like instruments pay a minimal amount of interest, making growth limited.

Does cash protect again inflation?

No, the minimal amount of interest may not outpace inflation.

Does cash provide stability, aka principal preservation?

Yes! That's why you hold cash. It's your stable rock for when the rest of your investments are moving up, down, and all around.

Does cash offer liquidity?

Yes! This is the other reason you hold cash. Sometimes you need access to your money quickly, and cash is great for that. You should have easy access to most cash-like instruments, but be aware of any restrictions, such as a contract stipulation that you can't access the instrument within the first six months without penalty, that type of thing.

KEY TAKEAWAYS

In this chapter, you got a crash course in investing essentials.

You learned the three reasons why you should invest:

1. To grow your money, cha-ching!
2. To keep up with rising costs in your daily life.
3. To keep more money in your pocket via tax efficiency.

And you also learned about the three main asset classes—stocks, bonds, and cash—with a breakdown of the pros and cons of each. In summary:

- Stocks give us the highest growth potential but have the highest risk.
- Bonds balance out the risk by providing a steady stream of income in the form of interest payments but limit growth potential.
- Cash provides stability and flexibility but no growth.

Now that you have a grasp of the essentials, we're going to dig deeper into how to invest like the pros. The key is to use a combination of these investments to create balance. In the next chapter, we'll look at how to do that through diversification.

CHAPTER 7

INVESTING
LIKE A PRO

September 15, 2008. I'm working at a financial institution in northern New Jersey. I head to lunch to grab a bite before my afternoon appointments. When I step back into the office, the stock market is plummeting. Lehman Brothers is collapsing, and every financial market in the world spins into a panic. The next few days are hectic. Rows of clients line up outside our doors because they want to talk to someone, anyone. They want answers. They want to sell their investments. They want to look someone in the eyes for reassurance.

My office was about fifteen miles from Manhattan. We had many Lehman Brothers employees as clients. I'm not talking about executives who made millions of dollars a year. I'm talking about people like you and me, only these people had worked for Lehman Brothers for more than 20 years. They fully believed in their company. They invested all their savings into Lehman Brothers stocks and bonds. They invested in what they knew: their company. The company that supported them and their families throughout the years. When Lehman Brothers went down, not only did these people lose their jobs, but they also lost the wealth that had taken them decades to build.

I watched clients cry in my office while I read them their account balances. My weak effort to console them fell on deaf ears. We both knew the truth. There was nothing I or anyone could do to get their life savings back. Talking to me was another thorn in their side. I heard this time and time again during the next few weeks: "You're so young; you have your whole life to work. I've lost everything, and I don't have time to make it back." I was twenty-five years old. They were right. I will never forget their faces, those conversations, and the long hours. I felt hopeless for them. I was no longer asking financial planning questions; I was asking life-changing questions. "Do you have any family members that can help you?" That's why I wholeheartedly believe in asset allocation and diversification. Consistent execution of these concepts will not only help you build your wealth, but you will also keep your wealth.

Stocks, bonds, and cash offer benefits, but no single investment can fit all your needs. It's time to introduce the ideas of asset allocation and diversification. Consistent execution of these concepts will not only help you build your wealth; it will help you *keep* your wealth. Asset allocation and diversification can be summed up with the age-old idiom, "Don't put all your eggs in one basket." You don't want to rely on one type of investment to determine your financial success.

MANAGING RISK

Asset allocation and diversification are strategies to manage risk. Since the financial markets are forward looking, it's impossible to predict future performance. This makes managing risk critical to your financial success. Investing is not gambling if you understand how to effectively manage risk. I'll give you a brief backdrop of key fundamental concepts without going too deep. Stay with me, grab another latte, let's geek out together for a moment.

Risk falls into two main categories: systematic and unsystematic risk. Systematic risk is also known as "volatility, market risk, and undiversifiable risk. It's unpredictable and impossible to entirely avoid. An example of systematic risk is the Great Recession of 2008. All economies and financial markets globally were negatively impacted by the recession. With financial markets all over the world unstable, there was no place to hide. As an investor, you can't completely avoid that type of risk because you can't predict major global or economic events. Trust me. I asked my Magic 8-Ball. The answer: Don't count on it. Although you can't predict these events or completely shelter yourself from this risk, you *can* minimize some of the effects through smart *asset allocation*, which we'll dive into in a moment.

Unsystematic risk is also known as specific risk or diversifiable risk. This type of risk is avoidable and can be reduced by diversification. There are two main types of unsystematic risk: company-specific risk and industry- or sector-specific risk.

Let's look at an example of company-specific risk. It's 2015 and you own Volkswagen stock. The stock price on April 15, 2015, is $244.80 per share.

Fast forward to September of the same year. Volkswagen is caught by the Environmental Protection Agency (EPA) with a "defeat device." This enables their US cars to cheat pollution standards. Volkswagen's stock price drops over 50% to a whopping $101.15 per share on September 27, 2015. Ouch.

Now let's look at an example of industry-specific risk. We'll use the airline industry during the 2020 coronavirus pandemic. It's 2019, and you own Delta Airline stock. The stock price on July 16, 2019, is $63.16 per share.

Fast forward to May 15, 2020. Shelter-in-place guidelines are set. Planes are flying almost empty, if at all. All travel-industry-related companies are negatively impacted, including Delta Airlines, whose stock is now trading at $19.19, over 60% lower in less than one year. Yikes.

If you invest in just one stock or one industry, events like these could *really* hurt your portfolio. By diversifying—owning a variety of stocks from different companies and different industries—you spread out your risk. Sure, you lose some money when these events happen, but it's only a small percentage of your portfolio, so it's not as painful.

ASSET ALLOCATION AND MODERN PORTFOLIO THEORY

So let's look at asset allocation. When you log into your accounts or grab a statement, there's usually a pie chart of your asset allocation front and center. Why do all investment companies want us to look at this colorful pie chart? The reason is simple. Asset allocation is the most important decision you can make when building your portfolio. But what is it exactly?

Asset allocation is an investment strategy that aims to balance the risk versus the reward of your portfolio. Having the optimal mix between stocks, bonds, and cash helps you have a smoother investing experience rather than riding the up and down waves that stocks alone can provide. You may not make as much money on the upside, but with buffers in place, such as adding bonds, you have protection on the downside.

This is the same strategy most professional money managers are using today. The best part is you can do this, too, all on your own. This whole concept of asset allocation is the genesis of modern portfolio theory (MPT). I'm going to briefly explain MPT so you understand the historical data and math backing this theory up, but if you don't care and just want to take my word for it, feel free to skip ahead to the Target Asset Mixes section. And if MPT gets your heart pumping and you want to read more, knock yourself out and have fun doing your own research, too.

Okay, MPT. Stick with me for a moment. Don't worry, there are no tests.

MPT was pioneered by Harry Markowitz in the 1950s, and he ended up winning a Nobel Prize in Economics for his work on it. MPT uses a mathematical framework that illustrates the optimal mix between stocks, bonds, and cash. Within MPT comes the efficient frontier. Thanks to these math geeks, there are optimal portfolios that illustrate the highest expected return for a defined level of risk. They examined a variety of factors and found that taking on more risk *doesn't* equal higher returns. Say what? Yup. That's right.

On the efficient frontier, you are efficiently investing. Meaning every time you increase the risk factor, such as buying more stock, you're getting rewarded. When you unnecessarily add risk, your portfolio becomes inefficient. This explains why having a portfolio of 100% stocks isn't ideal. Growth sounds great, but stocks are volatile. By adding bonds and cash into the mix, you can cushion downturns, ending up with higher returns in the long run. When you fall off the efficient frontier, you begin taking on too much risk without getting rewarded. Boo that strategy, right?

Although asset allocation won't guarantee protection against losses or even increase your returns, your overall risk is decreased. It's the balancing act of how you can participate in the upside of the market while minimizing the downside. Essentially, your potential reward based on the risk you take has been figured out. Thank you, math geeks. Woo-hoo! And phew, right? I'm going to stop talking about MPT. You were about to throw this book out. I get that.

TARGET ASSET MIXES

Based on MPT, there are hypothetical portfolios you can use as a guideline. Let's look at some of these hypothetical portfolios, which are called Target Asset Mixes (TAMs).

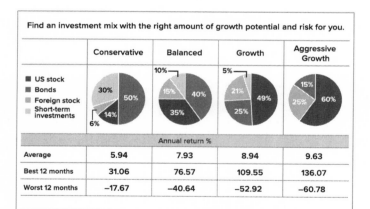

Find an investment mix with the right amount of growth potential and risk for you.

	Conservative	Balanced	Growth	Aggressive Growth
■ US stock ■ Bonds ■ Foreign stock ■ Short-term investments	30% 50% 14% 6%	10% 15% 40% 35%	5% 21% 49% 25%	15% 25% 60%
Annual return %				
Average	5.94	7.93	8.94	9.63
Best 12 months	31.06	76.57	109.55	136.07
Worst 12 months	−17.67	−40.64	−52.92	−60.78

Data source: Fidelity Investments and Morningstar Inc., 2020 (1926–2019). **Past performance is no guarantee of future results.** Returns include the reinvestment of dividends and other earnings. This chart is for illustrative and educational purposes only. Target asset mixes offer different risks and return characteristics to help you meet your goals. You should choose your investments based on your unique situation. It is not possible to invest directly in an index. Time periods for best and worst returns are based on calendar year. Hypothetical value of assets held in untaxed portfolios invested in US stocks, foreign stocks, bonds, or short-term investments. Stocks, foreign stocks, bonds, and short-term investments are represented by total returns of the IA SBBI US Large Stock TR USD Ext 1/1926–1/1987, Dow Jones Total Market from 2/1987–12/2019; IA SBBI US Large Stock TR USD Ext 1/1926–12/1969, MSCI EAFE 1/1970–11/2000, MSCI ACWI Ex USA GR USD 12/2000–12/2019; US Intermediate-Term Government Bond Index from 1/1926–12/1975, Barclays Aggregate Bond from 1/1976–12/2019; and 30-Day T-Bills.

Starting from the left, look at the hypothetical Conservative TAM. A Conservative portfolio is made up of 20% stocks, split between US and foreign companies, 50% bonds, and 30% cash. The average annual return in a Conservative portfolio is roughly 6%.

As you move from left to right, you increase your stock exposure (how much money you have in stocks) in return for potential growth. The average growth of an Aggressive Growth TAM is over 9%.

Even though you increase your stock exposure, you also increase your risk. This is illustrated by the worst twelve-month returns and the worst consecutive five-year returns. This is why you need to apply the appropriate asset allocation to your specific goals.

FIGURING OUT YOUR ASSET ALLOCATION

How do you go about figuring out your asset allocation? I'm glad you asked.

Asset allocation is based on three main factors:

1. Your goal's time frame. When do you plan on using the money?
2. Your tolerance to risk. How comfortable are you with market fluctuation? Do you lose sleep when your accounts' values go down?
3. Your current financial situation. How likely are you to touch this money before your desired time frame? Do you have an emergency fund established? Will you be forced to sell and abandon your investment strategy if you need cash quickly?

Intentionally thinking about these three factors will help you determine your asset allocation.

Let's look at an example of investing for retirement.

1. YOUR GOAL'S TIME FRAME

When do you plan on using the money?

You plan on using the money 30 years from now.

2. YOUR TOLERANCE TO RISK

How comfortable are you with market fluctuation? Do you lose sleep when your accounts' values go down?

You are comfortable taking on a lot of risk because you don't have a large balance in your retirement account yet. The market swings won't feel big since your account value is small. You also feel behind from where you should be, so your focus is growth.

3. YOUR CURRENT FINANCIAL SITUATION

How likely are you to touch this money before your desired time frame? Do you have an emergency fund established? Will you be forced to sell and abandon your investment strategy if you need cash quickly?

You have an emergency fund and other sources of money you can touch before you would need to access this account.

Based on these answers, you should consider an Aggressive Growth portfolio that has 85% stock exposure.

Here's another example. Let's say you're saving for a down payment on a home. Your asset allocation will be different from your retirement account. What should your ideal asset allocation look like?

1. YOUR GOAL'S TIME FRAME

When do you plan on using the money?

You plan on using the money 6 years from now.

2. YOUR TOLERANCE TO RISK

How comfortable are you with market fluctuation? Do you lose sleep when your accounts' values go down?

You are new to investing. You are not that comfortable with risk. You are also afraid to lose any of the money you've already saved.

3. YOUR CURRENT FINANCIAL SITUATION

How likely are you to touch this money before your desired time frame? Do you have an emergency fund established? Will you be forced to sell and abandon your investment strategy if you need cash quickly?

You are currently building your emergency fund. You had one, and then you needed to use some of the money.

With these answers, you may fall somewhere between a Conservative and Balanced TAM. When you're in between two strategies, it's a good time to listen to your gut. You want to believe in your strategy. Let's say you invest in a Balanced TAM. The market experiences a downturn. You abandon your strategy and panic sell your portfolio. In this case, you would've been better off investing in a Conservative TAM.

In figuring out your risk tolerance, I would look at how you are in everyday life. Are you a risk taker? You can also revisit your money past. If you've been prone to keeping your money safe in cash, I wouldn't jump into the deep end of the pool right away. Do what makes you comfortable. Pace yourself, and as time goes on, you'll be able to feel out your comfort zone. You are embarking on an investment journey after all. As you get more experience, your comfort level with investing will increase and you'll start to learn who you are as an investor. It's like anything else in life, talking about or studying will only get you so far. Taking action will give you the best experience that you can continue to learn from and adapt.

PERSONALIZE IT!

Okay, take a deep breath. Time for an emotional check-in. How are you doing? I think you're doing great! We should high-five. Or I guess you can just high-five yourself. But whatever you do, acknowledge the fact that you're becoming a savvy investor! Since you're on a roll, I want to share examples from our main characters to help this all really sink in and show you how asset allocation can be personalized for different goals. Later, in Chapter 10, I'll go into more detail about how to apply all these concepts and personalize each of your own goals. For now, these examples will get you into the practice of thinking about asset allocation.

JESSICA'S HOME SWEET HOME BUCKET

Jessica would love to be in a position where she could put a down payment on a home in 7 years.

1. Goal's time frame

Jessica will need the money in 7 years.

2. Tolerance to risk

Jessica is comfortable with some risk since she doesn't need the money for several years.

3. Current financial situation

Jessica has an established emergency fund and won't need to touch this money.

Asset Allocation

Balanced Portfolio: 50% stocks, 40% bonds, 10% cash.

Why

Jessica is comfortable with taking risk because she doesn't need the money soon. If she kept the money in cash, it would earn little interest and she wouldn't see much growth. A Balanced portfolio is a good middle-of-the-road path that will help her grow her money while taking on a level of risk she's comfortable with.

ASHLEY'S DREAM JOB BUCKET

Ashley would love to start her own business. This is truly her dream.

1. Goal's time frame

Ashley is planning on fully transitioning out of her full-time job within the next 10 years.

2. Tolerance to risk

Ashley is comfortable taking risk because she doesn't have money saved for this goal yet. She will be contributing toward this goal every month and wants to leverage her money.

3. Current financial situation

Ashley has an established emergency fund and won't need to access this money.

Asset Allocation

Balanced Portfolio: 50% stocks, 40% bonds, 10% cash.

Why

Ashley doesn't have a large sum of money she can dedicate to this goal right away. She will be making contributions and investments toward this goal every month. She is willing to take risk since she will be risking a small dollar amount at first. She is also willing to take risk to increase her chances of achieving her goal within her designated time frame.

MIKE AND SARAH'S HEY HEY VACAY BUCKET

Mike and Sarah want to go on vacations every year. This is definitely a priority for them.

1. Goal's time frame

They plan on using this money within the next year.

2. Tolerance to risk

Their tolerance for risk is extremely low. They know they will spend this money soon and don't want to take any risk.

3. Current financial situation

Mike and Sarah have an established emergency fund and won't need to touch this.

Asset Allocation

All cash.

Why

Preserving the principal is the most important consideration since they're going to spend this money in the next couple of years.

BREAKING DOWN DIVERSIFICATION: THE WONDERFUL WORLD OF STOCKS

Asset allocation—finding the optimal mix of stocks, bonds, and cash—is our starting point. Within those three asset classes is an entire universe of options. Enter diversification. We'll start with how to diversify stocks.

Let's talk shop. We discussed unsystematic risk earlier, which is also known as specific or diversifiable risk. This type of risk can and should be avoided. We know that although stocks offer the most growth potential, they also come with the most risk. When you build a portfolio, you need to own a variety of stocks so you're not placing bets.

> **Empowered Planning Golden Rule:** Avoid owning concentrated stock positions.

There are multiple definitions of "a concentrated position" out there. I define it as owning a stock that represents 10% or more of your total portfolio. A concentrated stock position exposes you to high risk. Your financial wellness is now reliant on the success or failure of a single company. Scary. You will never do that, right? Okay, good. Just checking.

Beyond avoiding concentrated positions, you also want to avoid owning too much of the same type of stock. The financial industry as a whole helps investors identify stock variety through something called style boxes. This concept was created by financial analytics firm Morningstar, Inc. In the interest of time, I won't go into more detail about its origin, but feel free to check it out. I'm going to walk you through these style boxes, and this will help you better understand how to invest.

Not all stocks are alike, so the Morningstar Style Box™ is split into nine categories to help illustrate the characteristics of a stock. Take a look.

Morningstar Style Box™
Equity Style Box

	Value	Blend	Growth
Large			
Medium			
Small			

Stocks are broken down by two main characteristics: size and style. The vertical axis represents the size of the stock. The horizontal axis represents the style of the stock.

STOCK SIZE

Sizes are broken down by market capitalization. All that means is stocks are separated by the total value of all a company's shares of stock. Here's a breakdown.

- Large-cap stocks have market capitalizations of $10 billion or more. Think S&P 500 companies—for example, Apple and Johnson & Johnson.
- Mid-cap stocks usually have market capitalizations between $2 billion and $10 billion. Think of the company Yeti—they

make coolers, coffee travel mugs—you've probably seen them around. You are less likely to be familiar with mid- and small-size stocks because they are not yet household brand names.

- Small-cap stocks typically have market capitalizations between $300 million and $2 billion. The definition of small-cap stocks could change slightly depending on who's talking, but this is the general idea.

The reason these size distinctions are made is because large-cap stocks behave differently than smaller-cap stocks. The long-term performance of small-cap stocks can be appealing, but they come with more risk. When the economy experiences a crisis, such as the financial crisis in 2008 or the COVID-19 pandemic of 2020, small-cap stocks suffer. These companies don't have access to as many resources as large-cap stocks do, such as the ability to raise capital quickly or strong brand names that are widely recognized.

For example, let's take Coca-Cola versus HNH. HNH is a fictitious small company that sells baby products. HNH are also the initials of my children; see how creative I can get? You can find a Coke in almost every country around the world. If Coca-Cola exists everywhere, how much more can it grow? HNH, on the other hand, is up and coming. It offers its baby products in select stores and is rapidly expanding. It is looking to take its products overseas, and the stock's growth potential is huge. HNH is the way to go, right? Grow your money! But wait. HNH could encounter many obstacles along the way before you make huge profits. During HNH's expansion efforts, it can run into legal and trade agreement issues, access to capital problems, and so forth, so the risk is higher for you as the investor.

The point here is, you want to own a mix of different stock sizes, but the smaller the stock size, the higher the risk.

STOCK STYLE

A stock's style is illustrated on the horizontal axis of the style box. The style of a stock is defined by either value, growth, or a blend of the two. I'm going to give you a rundown, but keep in mind, you don't need to become an expert. If you want to go deeper, that's always an option, but if you want an easy version of this, it exists. In the next chapter, I'll show you simplified ways to diversify. For now, I want you to build a baseline understanding of where these lingo and jargon come from so you can glide through the next chapter. You're doing great, by the way!

Growth Stocks

Think of companies like Amazon and Google. Investors (you) buy growth stocks because you expect them to grow faster than other companies. When growth is the priority, companies reinvest earnings back into themselves to further their growth and market reach. Whether that reinvestment is in research and development, equipment, expanding workforce, and so on, they're on a fast track for growth. Get out of the way!

Since they offer higher growth potential, they are considered riskier than value stocks. They are also more expensive, meaning there's a built-in premium to own these stocks in the first place. You may be slightly overpaying to purchase growth stocks, but your hope is that they grow even higher.

Value Stocks

Value stocks are selling at a "value," or discount. Think of shopping at Nordstrom versus Nordstrom Rack. You can get trendy outfits at Nordstrom, but it'll cost you. Or you can head to Nordstrom Rack. You'll spend more time treasure hunting, but you'll leave with some extra dollars in your pocket. Value investors look for bargains. They believe the market will recognize the company's true value in the future. This will send the stock price higher, and the investor will make a profit. Therefore, value stocks tend to be less expensive than growth stocks.

Another unique characteristic with value companies is they may not prioritize growth as their main agenda. They may offer a nice dividend to reward investors for owning their stock. Paying dividends is common for value stocks but not a set rule. Some examples of value stocks are McDonald's Corporation and Verizon Communications.

Remember, these are all characteristics but not always true. The market is forward looking; things change fast. As we know now, the Magic 8-Ball can't predict market returns.

DOMESTIC VERSUS INTERNATIONAL

You also want to diversify between domestic and international stocks. Domestic stocks, US stocks, are considered less risky than international stocks. The majority of your stock exposure should be domestic, but you want to sprinkle in international stocks. This will help decrease the domestic economic risk to your portfolio and allow you to participate in the upside of international markets. Double win!

International stocks are not just one category. You have large, well-established, international economies such as Japan and Germany, but you also have emerging or developing markets such as India and Brazil. Emerging markets bring higher potential return and higher risk. They may have unstable currencies, inaccurate financial reporting, and so forth. Remember, don't place bets.

BREAKING DOWN DIVERSIFICATION: ALL THINGS BONDS/FIXED INCOME

Next up, we have bonds. Did you know the bond market is much larger than the stock market? No, right? Why would you know that? Bonds are boring. But that's why you want to own them. Bonds, fixed incomes, are usually brought up when people are getting ready to retire or living in retirement. Bonds provide stability and pay you a stream of income, which means you should absolutely own some.

Bonds are categorized in a style box like stocks. See the illustration below.

Morningstar Style Box™
Fixed Income Style Box

	Short	Interm.	Long
High Quality			
Medium Quality			
Low Quality			

Bonds are broken down by two main characteristics: quality and duration. The vertical axis represents the quality of the company issuing the bonds. The horizontal axis represents the time frame in which the bonds will mature. Let's explore these further.

QUALITY/CREDIT RISK

Bonds are broken down by their quality and for good reason. All bonds are not created equal, and the differences in quality shed light on that immediately. The quality rating tells you how able the issuer will likely be to repay you.

Think about it like this: When you take out a home mortgage, the lender will run your credit. The lender will offer you an interest rate and terms that are reflective of the risk they are taking by lending you money to purchase the home. The lower your credit score, the higher the interest rate will be from the lender. This is the premium you are paying to borrow money with less-than-ideal credit. Just like we have three main credit bureaus that monitor our personal credit scores, there are three main credit-rating agencies that evaluate bond issuers. They are Moody's, Standard & Poor's, and Fitch. These agencies rate the financial health of the issuer and their ability to repay the bonds. They use letter ratings to illustrate their findings. You don't need to know all the ratings, but you do need to know if the bonds are considered investment grade (high to medium quality) or noninvestment grade (low quality), also known as junk.

Investment Grade

An investment-grade bond is considered to carry low default risk. Investment-grade bonds are typically large companies that we've heard of, such as Disney or the US government. The quality ratings of these bonds range between AAA to BBB−. Again, it's not important to memorize all of this; you can simply ask if a particular bond or fixed-income investment is considered investment grade or not.

Investment-grade bonds will pay less interest and preserve your initial investment. US government bonds usually set the standard for the interest rates companies are willing to offer. Since the government can literally print money, they have no risk of defaulting. Although a company may be healthy and well known, they do not have a magic money-making machine. Therefore, you increase your risk by purchasing a specific company's bond or even the bonds of a state or local municipality. This forces them to offer a higher interest rate payment than what a similar US government bond will offer. Otherwise, you as the investor would just stick with US government bonds; there'd be no incentive for you to take on extra risk.

Noninvestment Grade, AKA Junk Bonds

Noninvestment-grade bonds, or junk bonds, have ratings below BBB– and must pay higher rates of interest to attract investors. This is important to know because as you start looking at bonds to invest in, you may perk up when you find a bond that's paying a higher rate of interest. Warning! The issuer must pay more because of the potential default risk. The higher the risk associated with a bond, the more volatile they become. These high-risk bonds can bounce around in value like stocks. For the purpose of using bonds to serve as a counterpart to the stocks you own, you should stick to investment-grade bonds. If you own any junk bonds, they should be a small portion of your overall bond exposure.

DURATION/TERM, AKA TIME FRAME

Next up, we have the bond term. When does the bond mature, come due, or pay out? How long do you have to wait? This is illustrated on the horizontal axis of the style box.

Let's say your two BFFs, Linda and Kelly, each ask to borrow

$500 from you. And yes, you have two BFFs because you're that awesome.

Linda says she can pay you back in 1 year, and Kelly says she can pay you back in 3 years. You offer Linda the $500 if she can pay you $550 by next year. You offer Kelly the $500 if she can pay you $700 in 3 years.

There's less risk involved lending the money to Kelly since she'll pay you back in 1 year. This is exactly how bonds work. The longer the duration of the bond, the more interest the issuer will have to pay you since you are taking on more risk.

A bond's duration is categorized as either short term, medium term, or long term.

Short Term

Typically, a bond that matures within the next 2 years is considered to be short term. A short-term bond will pay less interest than a similar bond that comes due in 5 or more years because you have less risk as the investor.

Medium Term

Medium term typically means a maturity between 2 and 10 years. This is a wide range, so you get more interest than you would with a short-term bond but also aren't locked into a long time frame. This can be a sweet spot depending on the purpose of the bond relative to your overall investments. For example, let's say cash is paying you 1% interest, and you want to earn more than that. A bond coming due in 15 years would pay you 5% interest, but you don't want your money tied up that long. So you go out looking for a medium-term bond and find one that'll pay you 2% for 5 years. That option works great because you're earning more than you would in cash (at 1%) without having to tie up your money for 15 years (at 5%).

Remember that you don't need to become a bond master. You just need to know the fundamentals. Keep going. You're doing great! You're kicking investment butt right now. Big time. Big time butts. Let's keep that in context, please.

Long Term

Long term typically means a bond that matures in 10 or more years. Long-term bonds carry higher risk since you are relying on the company being able to repay you way down the line. There are other risks involved, such as interest rate risk and reinvestment risk. I'm not going to get into those details because I want to keep it high level, and it's unlikely long-term bonds would be an appropriate investment option for you. If you decide to invest in them, definitely do more homework outside of this book.

CASH-LIKE INVESTMENTS

I would simply use common sense when investing in cash-like instruments. If something sounds too good to be true, it probably is. For example, if cash in your checking account is paying you 1% and you see an offer for a savings account that would pay you 4%, I wouldn't rush to move my money over. That would be a red flag to me. Why would they be able to pay so much more? Check out what the terms are and if you can freely move your cash around.

If you want to hold cash for emergencies or part of a bigger investment, you want it to be liquid. A money market fund is a type of mutual fund that invests in fixed income and is short term and high quality. Its objective is to preserve your principal while earning a nominal rate of interest. This could be a great option for your emergency fund but not advantageous for achieving your long-term financial goals.

JOURNAL EXERCISE

Now it's your turn! Do a practice run of figuring out the rough asset allocation for one of your goals. You don't need to determine specific percentages right now, and this isn't set in stone. You'll personalize your asset allocations to all your specific goals in Chapter 10. For now, just decide what target asset mix would be best. This will give you a starting point from which you can adjust and get more specific.

Goal Name: _____

1. Goal's time frame

2. Tolerance to risk

3. Current financial situation

Desired Asset Allocation: _____

Why: _____ (You always want to know your why behind your chosen target asset mix. This is particularly handy when you're working through changes to your situation.)

KEY TAKEAWAYS

In this chapter, we learned that to personalize your asset allocation with your goals, you should look at three main factors:

1. Your goal's time frame. When do you plan on using the money?
2. Your tolerance to risk. How comfortable are you with market

fluctuation? Do you lose sleep when your accounts' values go down?

3. Your current financial situation. How likely are you to touch this money before your desired time frame? Do you have an emergency fund established? Will you be forced to sell and abandon your investment strategy if you need cash quickly?

We then discussed the importance of diversification—getting a good mix of different types of stocks and bonds in order to manage risk.

Now that you're becoming a savvy investor, we'll look at investing strategies in the next chapter and how you can tackle all of this in the easiest way possible. If your heart starts to race and you feel anxious, just remember that's excitement in an unorganized fashion. Once you put your plan in place, the anxiety will fizzle away. You will move to clarity and motivation. That's where we're headed! Once you've completed this step, you're more than half-way done with creating the lifestyle you want for yourself. Get through this part. People talk about change and growth. You are doing it. Treat yourself to dinner with some friends. You totally earned it!

CHAPTER 8

CHOOSING YOUR INVESTMENT STRATEGY

Before I started writing this chapter, I wanted to see what it's like to be you. I wanted to see what answers were out there. I did what we all do: I googled it. I googled the concepts, terms, and products I'll discuss in this chapter. I sifted through five publications from reputable sources on each topic. I have to tell you, I WAS BORED. I struggled to finish this little project because what I read was complicated, dry, and smothered in financial jargon. I drank way too much coffee to try and help the situation, but it wasn't doing the trick. I even gave myself a little slap on the face to stay awake. This stuff got seriously boring.

Managing your investments shouldn't be taken lightly. This investing stuff is crazy important to your life, but it doesn't need to be boring or so complicated it leaves your head spinning. We are trying to avoid information paralysis; that helps no one. We want to turn information into action. If you want to get into the weeds and immerse yourself in building your own portfolio, have at it.

The world is your oyster full of boring legal and financial terms. But for the rest of us who want to learn how to turn knowledge into action, let's keep it simple. You can take advantage of the tools and products out there right now. You can leverage your money to earn money, pay less in taxes, and have a working knowledge of investment opportunities without being an expert. I'll show you how to invest with confidence using a hands-off approach. Time to move from confusion to clarity.

BUILDING YOUR INVESTING STRATEGY

As you approach investing, there are tips you can follow, but it'll take real-world practice to work out the right strategy for you. You now have a working knowledge of the importance of asset allocation, but in order to turn that knowledge into actionable investing, you'll need to make a few decisions. I'm going to break down these decisions into five categories to keep this clear and simple.

1. MOST COMMON INVESTMENT VEHICLES

There's an entire universe of investment vehicles available. I'll give a snapshot of the most common ones so you can block out all the extra noise.

2. INVESTMENT PHILOSOPHIES

This portion is specific to investing in mutual funds and exchange-traded funds only. There are two main schools of thought. I'll break down the differences to help you prioritize what truly matters to you.

3. REBALANCING

Your investments will move as the markets shift. You want to understand how to make changes as your investments change.

4. INVESTMENT APPROACH

Will you take a hands-on or hands-off approach to investing? Let's set you up for success. You want to be realistic for how involved you want to be on a day-to-day basis.

5. FEES AND TAXES

Fees and taxes are boring, yes. But understanding fees and being tax savvy can save you money—not boring. It's important to be aware of how these work into your overall big picture.

Let's get started!

INVESTMENT VEHICLES

In the last chapter, we went through an overview of stocks and bonds, and now, we're going to dive into more specifics, looking at how to invest in these two asset classes. We'll look at three main methods: individual stocks, individual bonds, and mutual funds and exchange-traded funds.

INDIVIDUAL STOCKS

Individual stocks can be really fun to play with, or they can take you down a rabbit hole that has no clear way out. This is truly based on personal preference. You can buy an individual stock in a brokerage account. (I'll talk more about this in Chapter 11.) Buying individual stocks, keeping in mind your diversification goals, is the most difficult route. It's a time suck. You need to become best friends with the stocks you own. This is not a set-it-and-forget-it strategy. You need to be passionate about researching and evaluating stocks for this to be a successful endeavor.

Let's say you're using a Balanced target asset mix. Your stock exposure will be somewhere in the 50% to 60% range. Proper diversification requires you to own dozens of stocks. You need to diversify between industries, company sizes, and countries. That means you are making decisions about all those companies on an ongoing basis. If this excites you, then I invite you try it out. If it doesn't, don't worry; you have other options that we'll get to in a bit, including mutual funds and exchange-traded funds, as well as professional help.

Companies like Charles Schwab and Fidelity Investments offer stock-screening tools. These allow you to search for stocks based on criteria you set. From there, you can do further research to analyze each company. If a few weeks go by and you aren't comfortable buying individual stocks, switch your strategy. If you feel uneasy about the stocks you did end up buying, switch your strategy. Be flexible and honest with yourself. There's no right answer. Much of this is getting to know yourself as an investor.

You may want to own individual stocks without actively managing your entire portfolio. Totally understandable. You can own stocks as a hobby. For example, let's say you love Lululemon. You spend your extra cash there and believe in the direction of the company. You can buy its stock for fun. You don't want the growth of that stock to dictate your ability to reach your financial goals, though. Easy solution: keep the dollar amount less than 5% of your total account value. If you make money, awesome; you're the smartest person in the world. And if you don't, no big deal. Your financial goals aren't tied to the success of that stock. Nobody has to know you're not the smartest person in the world, *wink wink*.

INDIVIDUAL BONDS

You can buy individual bonds in a brokerage account. You can buy them new or used. Buying a new individual bond is called a new issue. A new issue gives you the most transparency. Since the bond is literally new, all the terms outlined are accurate. Buying a used individual bond is done through the secondary market, and it's a bit more complicated. It comes with variables you need to evaluate, such as markups on the pricing and commissions, the bond issuer, the interest rate environment, reinvestment risk, and so on.

It's uncommon for an average investor to buy and sell individual bonds because of the extra layer of complexity. As you get older, like retirement age for example, you may want to explore owning individual bonds. Having stability in your portfolio and strategies geared toward paying income rather than growth may become a priority. For now, I wouldn't get caught up in all the details. No need to overcomplicate things just yet. Keep it simple.

MUTUAL FUNDS AND EXCHANGE-TRADED FUNDS

The most popular investment vehicles for people with limited time are mutual funds and exchange-traded funds (ETFs). Mutual funds and ETFs are made up of a basket of securities that you can buy or sell through a brokerage firm on stock exchange. They are an attractive option because of their cost, risk management, and accessibility.

Here are some quick differences between the two.

Mutual funds are the OG on the block, gaining popularity in the 1950s. Mutual funds are a great option for investors looking to own them over the long term. They trade at the end of the day based on the closing prices of the underlying stocks and bonds inside the fund. This is very different from how individual stocks trade. You can trade individual stocks throughout the day in real time or with criteria attached.

ETFs were created in the early 1990s. They are similar to mutual funds since they are also made up of a basket of securities. However, ETFs offer a variety of alternative asset classes, such as currencies (e.g., the US dollar) and commodities (e.g., coffee). ETFs are primarily passive investments. They typically follow a market index, such as the S&P 500, or a specific theme. For example, an ETF can focus on buying dividend-paying stocks or healthcare stocks; the list goes on. They trade similarly to stocks. You can trade them in real time or choose criteria for when a sell or buy order would be triggered.

One of the major benefits of mutual funds and ETFs is they offer easy diversification. In the last chapter, we talked about unsystematic risk, including company-specific and industry-specific risk. Diversified mutual funds and ETFs allow you to spread out your risk among many companies and industries, shielding you from risks associated with the bad judgment or bad luck of a single company or one industry.

However, simply owning mutual funds or ETFs doesn't necessarily make your portfolio diversified. Say what? Yes, it's true. Let's say you do a little research and buy three mutual funds to spread out your risk. The fund names are something like Blue Chip Growth, Large Cap, and US Growth. When you dig into their holdings, you discover they're all invested in one area of the market. Even though you've invested in three different mutual funds, you own mostly large US technology stocks. If the technology industry takes a hit, you're in trouble! Remember the Morningstar Style Box™ with the nine sections we looked at before? This is a place where that box comes in handy. You can use that box to check out where the mutual fund is mostly investing and ensure you're actually diversified.

Time for a quick check-in. How are you feeling? You are taking ownership of your financial well-being. Be proud! If you're starting to feel overwhelmed, don't worry. I want to remind you, investing is like learning another language. Becoming fluent will take time. Later on in the chapter, I will talk about cost-effective ways you can approach this if you want to be hands-off. I'm giving you the backdrop so you can make an informed, educated decision on how to move forward. You got this!

INVESTMENT PHILOSOPHIES

The investment philosophies I'm about to discuss only apply to investing in mutual funds and ETFs. If you're not going to invest in either of these, feel free to skip to the next topic: rebalancing. Within this type of investing, there are two main camps that churn up a lot of discussion: active versus passive management. The choice is based on personal preference. I'll share the differences between them and how you can decide what style is right for you.

An actively managed fund has an investment manager or team of people who make all the investment decisions. They research and analyze when to buy, hold, and sell the underlying securities. They make these decisions to meet the overall objectives of the fund. For example, let's say a mutual fund's objective is to buy small-sized US company stocks. The fund manager will look for companies that are undervalued with growth potential. This team of investment professionals will evaluate hundreds of stocks to determine which ones will perform the best. If a stock they own doesn't look attractive anymore, they'll make the decision to sell it.

With a passively managed fund (called a passive fund or index fund), there's no team of investment professionals who are looking at the underlying holdings to make decisions. The fund follows a market index (see the sidebar on indexes), with the process being automated. These funds exist because you can't directly invest in an index.

So what's the right answer? Active or passive investment management?

That was a trick question. Some investors believe passive management is the way to go, and other investors believe active management is better. There is an overwhelming amount of research dedicated to this topic. If you have trouble sleeping, research this. I guarantee sleep after a few pages.

To help sum it up, here are the main advantages of buying an index fund. First, you are removing the risk that an active manager's strategy will yield subpar results if their strategy is out of favor with the current market direction. Humans aren't perfect and can make mistakes. Second, index funds carry a lower cost than actively managed funds since they require little maintenance. This makes indexing a popular option for investors. With an index fund, you're letting the market do its thing without raising costs for human management.

The main disadvantage of an index fund is that since these funds are automated, they rely on market efficiency. If the fund is tracking the S&P 500, a price drop in some of the largest holdings can result in a steep decline in the value of the fund.

The main advantage of an actively managed fund is the opportunity to outperform the index. With this style of investing, you get a human edge. The fund managers may be able to pick up on trends that benefit the fund's growth. For example, they may see a stock is overvalued and proactively sell it before the market realizes. This can lead to better overall returns.

The main drawback is that actively managed funds come with higher fees since those managers need to be paid for their work. (I'll talk more about fees later on in this chapter.) The other disadvantage, mentioned above, is that humans aren't perfect. Fund managers can get it wrong.

REBALANCING

This is where I might hurt your feelings. It's time to set realistic expectations. In theory, rebalancing is easy. Let's take a look at Ashley's Dream Job Bucket. Her ideal asset allocation is a Balanced target asset mix of 50% stocks, 40% bonds, and 10% cash. As the stock market grows, so does her account balance. YAY! Her asset allocation is also shifting. Her stock funds have been growing rapidly—more rapidly than her bonds and cash. That means her stock exposure is now close to 70% of her total account. Ashley should sell off 15% to 20% of her stock funds and buy more shares of her bond funds. This would put her portfolio back at her ideal target asset mix of 50% stocks, 40% bonds, and 10% cash. Easy, right? Well, not so much. In reality, what most people do is nothing.

UNDERSTANDING INDEXES

A stock index measures the stock market as a whole or a specific area of the market. An index illustrates the general health of the stock market or the smaller segment the index represents. Indexes are used as benchmarks to measure the performance of a mutual fund or ETF.

Indexes commonly make news headlines: "Investors are happy today with the Dow Jones being up 2%." Or you may hear, "Investors are feeling a lot of uncertainty with the S&P 500 dropping over 300 points this morning." What are you supposed to do with this information? Freak out? Bury your head in the sand? No. Let it flow through you. Be informed. Take action if it's necessary.

Think about indexes like hearing the weather forecast. It's Wednesday, and the forecast calls for rain Saturday morning. Will you grab your umbrella, throw on your cute but overpriced rain boots? Of course not. You're not going to do anything with that information immediately. You learn the information, store it in your brain, and move on with your day. You'll reference it if a friend asks you to go hiking early Saturday morning. That's how I want you to feel about hearing these stock index headlines: aware and informed.

Although there are literally thousands of US stock market indexes, the most widely known are the S&P 500, the NASDAQ, and the Dow Jones Industrial Average. But what are they exactly? Many people get this confused. Stock indexes are a combined calculation of the underlying stocks. There are several ways stock market indexes can be calculated. I will only highlight the two most popular: market-cap weighted and price weighted. There's no quiz at the end of this, but this is how all investment performance is measured, so you should have a working knowledge around this.

Market-capitalization weighted simply means the stocks in an index are considered by their size, also known as their capitalization. The larger the company size, the bigger the emphasis it has inside the index. An example of a market-capitalization-weighted index is the S&P 500.

Price weighted simply means stocks with a higher share price have a larger weight within the index. An example of a price-weighted index is the Dow Jones Industrial Average (DJIA).

Here is a rundown of the three most referenced stock market indexes.

The Dow Jones Industrial Average

The DJIA is the oldest and most well-known index. It's a price-weighted index. It's made up of the thirty largest and most influential companies in the United States. Its performance is used as a barometer for how confident or pessimistic investors are feeling about the stock market. That's why you hear about "the Dow" in the news all the time. Examples of companies in the Dow are Walmart, Johnson & Johnson, and ExxonMobil.

S&P 500

The S&P 500 is supposed to represent the 500 largest US stocks. It is the most frequently used benchmark for mutual funds, ETFs, and professional money managers. Since it's market-cap-weighted, the top ten stocks represent over 25% of the index. Examples of top stocks are Google, Apple, and Facebook. Why does this matter? If any of the top ten companies are not performing well, the entire index will go down.

The NASDAQ Composite Index

The NASDAQ Composite Index is a broad-based stock market index, which is why it's referenced frequently by the media. It's market-cap weighted and holds more than 3,300 stocks. Roughly 50% of the index is made up of technology stocks.

To rebalance her account, Ashley has to sell her funds that are making the most money; they are her winners. She then has to buy more of the stuff that isn't making her money. Nobody likes to do this. Logically, rebalancing is easy to understand but emotionally challenging. Sell your winners and buy more of your losers? This is one of the hardest things to do in practice. We're not robots; we're humans. But rebalancing is necessary to manage the risk you are taking.

INVESTMENT APPROACH: HANDS-ON OR HANDS-OFF?

It's time to figure out if you want to do it yourself or assign the responsibility to a pro. If you want to hire a professional money manager to handle a stock portfolio for you, management fees usually start around 1% of your total account balance and have high minimums, such as $500,000 or more. I'll discuss using a cost-effective way to enlist the pros if you decide to invest in mutual funds and ETFs.

TACKLING THIS BY YOURSELF

You can do research, pick your investments, and rebalance throughout the year. If you enjoy it, go nuts. Have fun, but be strict about an execution timeline. Don't stay in research mode for long. The market moves fast, making last month's research outdated. You can use actively managed funds or index funds to build your portfolio. It's up to you to stick to your chosen asset allocation and make changes when necessary. You want control; you look at this like a hobby.

TACKLING THIS HANDS-OFF

Using a hands-off investment approach doesn't mean you have to pony up the big bucks. You want to match your goals with the appropriate asset allocation, then diversify. There is a cost-effective way to do this. There are mutual funds and ETFs that do this for you. They are called asset-allocation funds, and there are two main kinds:

1. Target asset mix funds
2. Target-date funds, aka age-based or life-cycle funds

These funds give you a diversified mix of investments. They are generally funds of funds rather than investing in individual stocks and bonds. I'll explain more. The asset-allocation fund will be made up of a variety of funds to create the target allocation. These funds will maintain the asset allocation over time. For example, if you select a balanced fund and its objective is to maintain a 50% stocks/50% bond mix, it will not change dramatically. If the stocks in the fund grow past 50%, the fund will be rebalanced automatically to maintain the 50/50 mix. Similarly, if the stocks decline and the bonds grow past 50%, the fund will be rebalanced to maintain the 50/50 mix. You don't have to rebalance anything by yourself. Phew, right?

Life-cycle or target-date funds will use a target date as a benchmark for when you intend to use the money. The fund will gradually become more conservative. For example, let's say you are looking at a 2030 target-date fund. As we get closer to the year 2030, the fund will decrease its stock exposure over time. You can easily tell what the fund is investing in by looking at its composition or holdings. This will tell you if the fund is invested in index funds, actively managed funds, individual stocks, and so forth.

Let's look at a target asset mix fund in a real-life scenario. Let's say you want to upgrade to a new home 10 years from now. Based on this timeline, your risk tolerance, and your current financial situation, you decide you want a growth portfolio with a 70/30 stocks-to-bonds mix. As time passes, the fund automatically rebalances itself so you don't need to build or maintain it. YAY! A couple of years after you first invest in the fund, you end up taking a promotion that's out of state. In your new city, housing prices are lower. You rerun your numbers and discover you're only 5 years away from your goal. This is great news. But it means you may want to decrease the amount of risk you're taking. In this instance, you need to take action. The fund will stay at the 70/30 stocks-to-bonds mix. You can exchange the fund into a new asset mix that works better for your situation, such as a 60/40 mix or 50/50 mix. That exchange doesn't happen automatically. That is driven by you.

Let's look at a target-date fund in a real-life scenario. Target-date funds have a year attached to their name. These funds are designed for investors who plan on using the money at a predetermined date. That's why these are popular for retirement goals. If you know you'll retire in 30 years and it's currently 2020, you select a life-cycle fund with a target date of 2050. These funds automatically decrease their level of risk as you get closer to the target date. You can use this for any of your financial goals if you know the date you need the money. You can set it and forget it!

Robo-Advisor

It's worth mentioning you can also use something called a robo-advisor. Unlike traditional investment management that requires high minimums, robo-advisors have low minimums and are offered at minimal fees (often less than 0.5%). Robo-advisors are automated investing services that use algorithms to manage an investment portfolio. Every major brokerage firm offers a robo-advisory service option, so go ahead and explore this option if it's attractive to you. Ask questions until you're comfortable enough to make a decision!

I like auto-rebalancing funds because although I'm interested in the financial markets, I'm juggling quality time with the kids, hubby, career, exercise, family, and friends. On top of that, I need my solo time to reflect and decompress. Solo time usually comes in the form of me locking myself in the bathroom and soaking in the tub. That way, if anyone comes looking for me, I can't help because my entire body is submerged under water. How could I possibly help you change a diaper right now? I would make a bigger mess. Ha! Try and argue with that one.

But seriously, for me, I don't want to spend my free time managing my portfolio and making trades. I know what I'll do. I'll come up with ideas, tell myself I should research further, and end up doing nothing. Boo that plan. I like hands-off. You can choose what works for you.

Time for a check-in. How are you feeling? Do you want to do this yourself, or are you ready to take the pro route? Whatever the answer is, it's the right answer. The point is that you have an opinion. This will lead to making decisions. You are all about action.

FEES AND TAXES

When investing, it's common to overlook fees and taxes, but they are incredibly important. You need to understand the environment you're playing in. Tax implications sound boring. Saving money and keeping more in your pocket sound fun. These are important elements of investing and carry consequences. However, taxes and fees should not dictate how you invest. They should be taken into consideration; they shouldn't drive all your decisions.

I'm going to keep this to the point. This is not everything you can learn about fees. Whatever areas you find interesting or have more questions about, explore them further. In Chapter 11, I'll review investment companies you can work with and things to consider when choosing. In the meantime, here is a quick snapshot of fees.

INDIVIDUAL STOCKS FEES

You can pay per trade or per number of shares, or it may be free. For example, if you buy one hundred shares of Nike, you may be charged one fee for the transaction, or the fees may be dependent on how many shares you purchased. If stock trading is free, you should understand how that company makes its revenue. If you have questions about the fees, ask.

INDIVIDUAL BONDS FEES

You can pay per trade or per size of the bonds you are trading. The price of the bond, not the commission fees, may reflect additional costs. If you have questions, ask the brokerage firm you are using.

MUTUAL FUNDS AND EXCHANGE-TRADED FUNDS FEES

Mutual funds come with two kinds of fees: transaction fees and expense ratios.

A transaction fee is a fee you pay to purchase a fund. These are no longer common, as most companies offer no-transaction-fee funds. If you're getting charged transaction fees, I would hit the brakes. Look somewhere else. There are too many other options that don't have these fees. If you're not sure about the costs associated with the fund you're looking to buy, ask.

An expense ratio is the annual fee shown as a percentage. This represents the investment management fee, recordkeeping, legal services, and so forth that all go into the management of the particular mutual fund or ETF. For example, let's say you're buying a mutual fund that invests in large US stocks. There's a ton of information readily available and accessible. A reasonable expense ratio for this category is under 1%. If you're buying an international stock fund, more research is required. The fund manager will need more resources to get the information needed to make buy and sell decisions on the underlying stocks. It would be reasonable for the expense ratio to be more than 1%.

Index funds have lower expense ratios. They are not being actively managed by a person or team. Index funds are tracking an index, making their expenses low.

ETFs come with two kinds of fees: transaction fees and expense ratios. The transaction fees for ETFs are similar to stock trading fees. Some companies offer a variety of them for free; others may charge per trade. The expense ratio fees function the same as for mutual funds. Poke around to make sure you understand the total cost.

TAXES

The taxation of your investments matters. You want to hold on to as much of your money as possible, right? Let's talk taxes, baby! I'll talk about retirement accounts in the next chapter. Right now, we are sticking with taxes you pay on nonretirement accounts.

Empowered Planning Golden Rule: Don't let the tax tail wag the investment dog.

What do I mean? Don't let the idea of paying taxes cloud your mind from making sound investment decisions.

Let's go through an example with rebalancing your portfolio. Easy in theory, difficult in reality. I was saving and investing for a down payment on a home. I was in a high-risk portfolio since my goal was years away. An international stock fund I owned grew fast. I knew I should sell off a chunk of it. I also knew I'd have to pay capital gains taxes close to $8,000. I didn't need to use the money right away. I thought, "Why sell it? It's only gone up; why pay taxes on money I'm not going to spend now?" Of course, the market took a downturn, and my gains on that fund were cut in half. Oh, it gets worse. I'm thinking, "I don't want to sell it now. I'll wait until it comes back and then sell it." The value continued to decline. I quickly learned I shouldn't be doing this on my own. It's emotionally challenging to sell your winners in the first place. On top of that, you have to pay taxes, too? Holding on to gains for too long can work against you. Paying the taxes isn't fun, but you are capturing your gains by selling when your investments are high. I'm going to give you a quick snapshot of common investing tax implications.

Short-term capital gains are when you sell an investment you've owned for less than twelve months for a profit. The profit is taxed as ordinary income.

Short-term losses can be used against short-term gains. Let's say you sell Fund A for a $6,000 profit after owning it for three months. At the same time, you sell Fund B for a $2,000 loss after owning it for six months. You pay $4,000 in short-term capital gains tax that year. If you have a short-term loss that is greater than your short-term gain, you can deduct it against a long-term gain.

If you have losses and no gains to offset them, you can use a maximum of $3,000 of capital losses per year to write off against income. If you have more than $3,000, you can carry that forward to the following tax year.

Long-term capital gains are when you sell an investment you've owned longer than twelve months for a profit. Long-term capital gains are taxed at a rate of 0%, 15%, or 20% depending on your taxable income and marital status. I'm not going to go through all the scenarios. Here's the middle of the road as of 2020: married couples who earn between $80,001 and $496,600 will have a capital gains rate of 15%.

Dividend income from an investment is considered qualified or nonqualified. Qualified dividends, which include those paid by US companies, are taxed at the long-term capital gains rate. Nonqualified dividends, such as those paid by real estate investment trusts (REITs), are taxed at the regular income rate.

Interest income from an investment is taxed as ordinary income. You will see this most often when you earn interest on savings accounts, CDs, money market funds, and bonds. For example, let's say you earn $100 in your savings account in the form of interest. In the eyes of the IRS and your home state, this is considered income. That $100 is added to your current year's income as if your employer gave it to you. Boo, right? People combat this by purchasing tax-free money markets and bonds. They can be federally tax-free or state- and local-tax-free.

INVESTING STRATEGIES IN ACTION

Okay, enough of that tax stuff! Let's see how our main characters are choosing to invest. Are they going to use a hands-on or hands-off approach?

JESSICA

Jessica definitely wants to be hands-off. She is excited to learn about creating financial goals, investing, and planning for retirement. She doesn't want to spend her free time making day-to-day investing decisions. Let's take a look at her goals and her investment strategies.

I Got Love for You Bucket

Jessica wants to go on a big vacation every year.

Her priority is to preserve the money.

Her target asset mix is 100% cash.

Her investment strategy is to buy a money market fund or open a high-yield savings account.

Big Things Are Coming Bucket

Jessica knows she will need a new car within the next 5 years. She also wants to be able to have a wedding if she meets the right guy.

Her priority is to preserve this money.

Her target asset mix is 100% cash.

Her investment strategy is to buy a money market fund or open a high-yield savings account.

Home Sweet Home Bucket

Jessica wants to buy a home. Her ideal time frame is 7 years.

Her priority is to grow her money without taking too much risk.

Her target asset mix is a Balanced portfolio: 50% stocks, 40% bonds, and 10% cash.

Her investment strategy is to buy a Balanced asset-allocation fund rather than a target-date fund. She wants the flexibility and control. She doesn't want a fund that will automatically change to become more conservative over time. She thinks this will motivate her to look at her investments regularly and keep her dream home top of mind.

Rockin' Retirement Bucket

Jessica plans on retiring in 30 years and is ramping up her savings.

Her target asset mix is Aggressive Growth: 85% stocks and 15% bonds.

Her investment strategy is to buy a life-cycle or target-date fund geared toward 2050. She loves the idea of a one-stop shop for this account. She wants to be more involved with her investments, but she is realistic. She has limited time and will be focusing on her shorter-term goals.

ASHLEY

Ashley also wants to be hands-off with her investment strategy. She wants to spend her free time growing her side business. The goal is to make that her full-time gig. Let's look at her goals and her investment strategy.

Wedding Extras Bucket

Ashley wants to have extra money set aside for her wedding. If they go over budget, she wants the flexibility to say yes. She will spend whatever money is left over on their honeymoon.

Her priority is safety.

Her target asset mix is 100% cash.

Her investment strategy is to keep this in her current savings account.

Future Condo Bucket

Ashley is thinking of buying a starter home or condo. She has the option to rent a place from a friend who is potentially relocating out of town. Renting this place would allow Ashley and her fiancé to boost their savings over the next 2 years. There's a lot of variables at play right now. She will know in six months if her friend's place will be available.

Her priority is safety.

Her target asset mix is 100% cash.

Her investment strategy is to keep this in her current savings account.

Dream Job Bucket

Ashley wants to transition into entrepreneurship full time in 10 years.

Her priority is to get invested.

Her target asset mix is a Balanced portfolio: 50% stocks, 40% bonds, and 10% cash.

Ashley's investment strategy is to use a target-date fund. She doesn't want to forget to change the asset allocation after a few years. Using a target-date fund gives her peace of mind.

Relaxation Retirement Bucket

Ashley loves her work and plans on retiring in 35 years. She has seen the impact of not being financially prepared.

Her priority is growth.

Her target asset mix is Aggressive Growth: 85% stocks and 15% bonds.

Her investment strategy is a target-date fund. She has access to these funds in her 401(k) plan at work. She currently owns six different target-date funds. She didn't realize this wasn't a good strategy. She thought by doing this, she was diversifying. She didn't realize there's a lot of overlap. Now she understands the purpose of these funds and is picking a target date that closely matches her ideal retirement year.

MIKE AND SARAH

Mike and Sarah are doing a mix between hands-on and hands-off. Mike can see himself doing this as a hobby in the future. He is so busy with his current business that it's not realistic for him to spend a lot of time on this right now, though. Mike wants to open a small brokerage account where he can put some savings and trade a few stocks and ETFs. Mike and Sarah are really interested in index funds. They are going to focus on indexing for their investment strategy.

Hey Hey Vacay Bucket

Mike and Sarah want to go on vacations every year.

Their priority is safety.

Their target asset mix is 100% cash.

Mike's investment strategy is a high-yield savings account. Mike has a great relationship with his bank because of his business account. They offer him this account along with flexibility.

Mini Me Bucket

Mike and Sarah are planning for a baby.

Their priority is to preserve this money.

Their target asset mix is 100% cash.

Their investment strategy is a high-yield savings account at Mike's local bank.

Future Presidents Bucket

Sarah wants to make sure they can support their children through college. They don't have kids yet but want to establish this savings routine now.

Their priority is growth.

Their target asset mix is Aggressive Growth: 85% stocks and 15% bonds.

Their investment strategy is a target-date fund that is 20 years out. They are going to use a college savings account. Sarah's company partners with an investment firm that offers the type of account that Sarah is comfortable using.

Retirement in Style Bucket

Although they will have separate accounts, their goals for this bucket of money are the same. Mike and Sarah want to save for retirement and not touch the money for at least 30 years.

Their priority is growth.

Their target asset mix is Aggressive Growth: 85% stocks and 15% bonds.

Mike's investment strategy is to choose his own index funds to create the asset allocation. He will rebalance this as needed. Sarah's investment strategy is to buy a target-date fund that is made up of index funds.

JOURNAL EXERCISE

Now it's your turn! Are you inspired to start investing on your own? Are you imagining all the ways you can assign this to someone else? Either way, make a decision. Not making a decision is still a decision; it's just a crappy one. The whole reason you are putting up with my sometimes-witty, sometimes-confusing jokes is because you want to take serious action toward reaching your money goals. Decide what kind of investor you are; you can change your mind later. I know I need to delegate the day-to-day management of my investments to an asset-allocation fund. I will drop the ball somewhere. I know this because I've tried. Here are questions to help you find what will work for you.

1. How much time a week do you want to spend making decisions on your investments? This is very different from reading and absorbing information. I'm not talking about how much time you want to spend learning. How much time are you going to spend making execution decisions. For example, should I buy, hold, or sell? Think about this in a weekly time frame. Usually, if someone says they'll do it once a month, that means never. It's not their fault. Life happens. This usually gets pushed to the bottom of the list because it requires undivided attention.

2. How interested in investing are you? You don't need to be an expert today. Do you see this as a hobby that you'd like to spend your time doing? Let's be real here.

3. What has your investing pattern looked like in the past? Lay it out there. Write this out like a timeline. When you do it like a timeline, you can see it clearly. No shame in the investing game. Just be honest. My timeline would look something like 4/1—I started researching some ideas. 4/7—I looked at my investments. 4/10—I thought about making changes. 6/1—I started researching some ideas. You know the rest.

KEY TAKEAWAYS

Here's what we learned in this chapter:

1. Stocks, bonds, mutual funds, and ETFs are the most common investment vehicles.
2. Passive management and active management are investment philosophies widely used today.
3. Rebalancing is important but difficult to do.
4. Decide what investment approach will work best for you. Do you want to be hands-on or hands-off?
5. Be aware of fees and taxes. Ask questions until you're comfortable.

Now that you have an idea of your investing strategy, it's time to look at one specific investing goal we all have to deal with: retirement.

.

CHAPTER 9

AWAKENING YOUR INNER RETIREE

Right now, there are 10,000 baby boomers retiring every day. Our country has never experienced this before. Many people retiring are shocked at the lifestyle changes they need to make to stay afloat financially. Someone retiring today would have been coming of age during the 1960s and 1970s. Think about that for a minute. Here's a few things that happened during that time in no particular order. You had the civil rights movement, the Vietnam War, the women's rights movement, and two horrifying assassinations: JFK and Martin Luther King Jr. We also can't leave out the first man on the moon, Woodstock, and Watergate.

It's not far-fetched to say many of these teenagers had an anti-big-establishment mentality. I'm not saying they started living off the grid, but they were interested in forming a new way of thinking and challenging the status quo. With this came innovation in every industry. Behind the scenes, pensions started to change; 401(k)s were introduced and not everyone got the memo. The hard truth is that how you receive income in retirement has been changing over the last 30 years. Many people don't start thinking about retirement until their early fifties. A common refrain among those staring down retirement is, "Why didn't somebody tell me this sooner?"

I'd like to share a story of two sisters, Linda and Sharon, to help illustrate this further. When I was working as a financial planner, I met Sharon, who was in her early sixties. She was incredibly sweet right from the beginning. Sharon was small in stature, had funky, short red hair, and was really nice. She was the kind of person you could open up to easily, but she also gave off this "don't mess with me" vibe. She was spunky, which I loved about her. Sharon never married. She worked as a hospital administrator her entire career. She owned her home free and clear. She'll receive a pension and Social Security once she retires and has investments to draw from. She always talked about her sister Linda in our meetings since they were so close. Linda was the stylish, adventurous sister. Linda and her husband frequently traveled overseas. They owned a few restaurants, had a beautiful home in a fancy neighborhood, and drove luxury cars. Sharon always bragged about Linda in a loving way.

A couple of years after I first met Sharon, Linda's husband passed away. Linda wanted to sit down with me to establish a financial plan. What I learned was devastating. Linda had little to no savings. She and her husband were leveraged on all their businesses and their home. She wasn't able to retire. I was shocked, especially as an outsider looking in. Linda had built this persona that she was living the high life from her successfully run businesses. Linda had to sell everything, the restaurants, her home, and her car, to free up cash. Linda had to move in with Sharon. Linda continues to work at one of her previous restaurants. She may never be able to stop working.

This is a harsh reality. Not everyone has the safety net of a sister or family member who can take them in if this were to happen. My hope is that you stay motivated about investing in your financial well-being. No one else will be there to do it for you. Something I always say when it comes to finances is, "People don't plan to fail; they fail to plan."

Today, the average millennial has less than $30,000 saved for retirement. Experts say you should have one times your salary saved by age 30. By age 40, you should have three times your salary. Where are you at right now? We are not taught about financial well-being in school, but you are learning now. You won't have to worry about any "Oh, crap!" moments when you get ready to retire because you're about to go through retirement boot camp. Strap up! It's time to play catch-up.

A TRIP DOWN RETIREMENT PAST

Previously, as generations of Americans moved into retirement, pensions and Social Security supported their lifestyles. In the 1970s, the average retirement age was 65, with the average life expectancy being age 67. Almost everyone had a pension. It was commonplace to work for one company for 30 to 40 years. After that, companies provided pensions that would pay close to your full salary. You put in 30 or more years. You live for a few years into retirement. You don't need to be a mathematician to see how this is simple for a company to handle.

Here's an example: Will worked for Jones Paper Co. from age 25 to his retirement at age 65. His average income over his forty-year career was $4,000 per month.

After retiring, his pension paid him $3,000 per month. Will also filed for Social Security at age 65, and his monthly benefit paid him $1,000 per month. So Will was able to receive his full income once he stopped working. Pretty sweet, huh?

Any money Will saved while working could be used for vacations, home improvements, inheritance for his children, and so forth. Will did not have to figure out how to turn his savings into a paycheck indefinitely.

RETIREMENT TODAY

As a generation, millennials are uber-focused on wellness, and we are living longer than ever before, especially women. We tend to live longer than our male counterparts, which proves we're a stronger species. Just kidding, but seriously, who's with me on that? Not only are we living longer, but we now have to fund our own retirements. Although pensions are still common among public service sectors (think education, hospitals, city, state, and federal jobs), according to a Willis Towers Watson retirement study, only 14% of *Fortune* 500 companies offered a pension plan to new hires in 2019. This pension offering is down from 59% among the same employers back in 1998.

Should we storm angrily in the streets and blame big companies and the government for this? Well, not exactly. Pensions are a huge risk to employers. Pensions promise to continually pay you a predefined amount of money in the future with an undefined end date. Companies take on all the risk. They need to accurately estimate how long you will live and the growth of pension investments over 30 or more years. Imagine how ugly this can get if they make inaccurate assumptions. Take a look at my home state of New Jersey. Their severely underfunded pension is creating insensitive tax hikes and has people fleeing the state en masse. If companies are forced to offer pensions because we can't do this ourselves, there will be serious consequences. Massive layoffs, decreased and fixed salaries, and less control over your money are a few immediate impacts.

Don't grab the tissue box for those tears just yet. This isn't all bad. Since we are in control of how much we save through our retirement plans—for example, 401(k)—we have flexibility. We can change jobs or take a career break to be home with kids, and we can bring our retirement plans with us. Pensions can serve as golden handcuffs. They tie us to one company. They have limited to no flexibility. Let's face it. We *LOVE* options. I can't find many people who are excited by the prospect of working for one company for 40 years.

Take me, for example. I loved my career as a financial advisor. It challenged me to think creatively and constantly expand my knowledge. But I didn't love traveling or being out of the house for fifty-plus hours each week. I would rush home, bathe my son, feed him, tuck him in, shovel dinner down my throat, collapse on the couch, and wake up to do it again. I wanted more time with family. So I went out on my own. With entrepreneurship came flexibility. But I lost someone looking out for my retirement. I don't have my matching contributions or extra perks. That's a tradeoff I willingly accept.

Blaming someone else for not having access to a pension isn't a solution. Hoping things will change isn't a plan. Companies don't want to put their profits toward paying us after we stop working for them. Shoot, we don't even want to do it for ourselves. Ouch, I know. Truth bombs can hurt.

SOCIAL SECURITY

Social Security shouldn't be forgotten. Did you just get sleepy eyes as soon as you read "Social Security"? It's latte time! I'll keep this brief. The Social Security benefit was created back in the 1930s by President Franklin D. Roosevelt to help alleviate the massive poverty rates among seniors following the Great Depression. Although Social Security exists, you shouldn't rely on this as your main source of income when you retire. The average monthly Social Security benefit in 2020 is $1,503 per month. That's about $50 a day to live on. Who can do that?

There are some public sector jobs that don't participate in Social Security. For the rest of us, we pay a percentage of our income into Social Security up to a wage base. The wage base is currently $137,700. So any income you make up to $137,700, you need to pay your portion of Social Security (6.2%), and your employer also pays 6.2% on your behalf. If you make more income than that, you don't contribute anything additional.

Social Security benefits are funded by a dedicated payroll tax, which, as workers, we pay into as we earn income. There is a risk that as baby boomers collect their Social Security payments, the current workforce won't be able to replenish the funds fast enough. Congress is constantly working on ideas that could help sustain Social Security payments. But there isn't anything concrete worth talking about right now. I'm better off guessing why my tantrum toddler is okay with having a sock on his right foot and not his left.

Now you know everything there is to know about the retirement landscape. You're basically an expert. So let's get into the specifics of what you really care about: *your* retirement journey.

AM I SAVING ENOUGH FOR RETIREMENT?

Your main income stream in retirement will be from money you stack away today. Many women that I take through my course are saving but have no idea if they're on track. Well, how do you know if you're saving enough? Although this isn't an exact science and opinions vary among financial professionals, here are some guidelines to reference.

First, you are aiming to have your annual cash flow in retirement equal 80% of your current income. This is assuming you don't want your lifestyle to drastically change once you stop working.

Check out these retirement savings goals by age, from Fidelity Investments:

- At age 30, you should have one times your salary in retirement savings.
- At age 40, you should have three times your salary in retirement savings.
- At age 50, you should have six times your salary in retirement savings.
- At age 60, you should have eight times your salary in retirement savings.
- At age 67, you should have ten times your salary in retirement savings.

If you don't have that yet, don't stress. I'm keeping it real with you. Your head can't be in the clouds with your livelihood on the line. These are guidelines to work toward. You don't need to compare yourself to other people. You do, however, have to start keeping score of your own progress.

So how do you get there? How do you make sure you have six times your salary by age 50?

> **Empowered Planning Golden Rule:** Save a minimum of 15% of your gross income toward retirement.

Saving a minimum of 15% of your gross income is a great place to start. In the next pages, we'll explore several retirement accounts you can use for these savings. I will go through features, benefits, and rules.

THE POWER OF COMPOUNDING INTEREST AND TAX DEFERRAL

Before we dive into the specifics of different retirement strategies, I want to start with two things all retirement accounts have in common: compounding interest and tax deferral.

I talked about compounding interest in previous chapters, and guess what? It's back. Einstein called compounding interest the eighth wonder of the world. And, well, he's freaking Einstein, so there's that. With compounding interest, all the money you earn can then be reinvested, earning you even more money as time goes by. Because of compounding interest, the sooner you start investing in your retirement, the better.

Investing is your superpower, right? What happens when we mix your superpower with tax deferral? I call it the magic sauce.

All retirement accounts offer the magic sauce of tax deferral while they're accumulating. I'll review how to avoid future taxes altogether in the Roth section later in this chapter. For now, let's focus on the power of tax deferral. Remember the example in the previous chapter surrounding taxes? You made $100 of interest in your savings account, and the IRS and state taxed it as ordinary income. To keep it simple, let's say after taxes you keep only $70 in your pocket. In your retirement accounts, regardless of what type, you keep the $100. You don't pay taxes on the earnings each year. You get to take that $100 and compound interest, which is *AMAZING*. Over time, the tax savings on this deferral can add up to thousands. This is a great way to have your money work on your behalf.

There's a variety of retirement accounts available to you, and it can feel overwhelming. Don't stress about doing it "right." Yes, you want to optimize all the benefits, but your main priority should be to simply do *something*. Move the needle forward, even if only a little. As long as you're participating in any type of retirement account, you're doing the right thing. You're getting the benefits of compounding interest and tax deferral. If you find yourself researching for too long, let that be a light bulb to stop. You don't need to become an expert. Taking action is more impactful than knowing everything. As you get more comfortable with the financial world, you can fine-tune your strategies.

With that in mind, let's take a look at the types of retirement accounts available.

INDIVIDUAL RETIREMENT ACCOUNTS

Individual retirement accounts (IRAs) come in two flavors: traditional IRA and Roth IRA. The IRS doesn't make these rules cut and dry. Surprised? Me neither. I am not going to get into all the details. If you want more information about a certain account, look it up on the IRS's website. They will have the most up-to-date, reputable information. You can also consult a tax advisor.

AM I ALLOWED TO CONTRIBUTE?

A traditional IRA doesn't have income limits on whether or not you can contribute. It does, however, limit your ability to deduct your contributions from taxes.

This is different from a Roth IRA. The IRS uses your current income to determine whether or not you can directly contribute to a Roth IRA. You can check out the IRS tables to see this year's limits.

If you don't qualify to directly contribute to a Roth IRA, you can do a *back-door contribution*. You contribute directly to a traditional IRA, you don't take any of the tax benefit (which I'll cover below), and then you immediately "convert" that money to a Roth IRA, making it a back-door contribution. Say what?

Of course, there are extras you may need to consider. I will not cover all of those. If you're interested in this, call your brokerage firm or tax advisor. Ask away.

HOW MUCH CAN I CONTRIBUTE?

For both a traditional IRA and Roth IRA, the maximum you can contribute is $6,000 in 2020 if you're under age 50.

You can put money in both a traditional and a Roth IRA. However, you can't contribute the maximum to both. Your total contributions cannot exceed $6,000 in 2020.

The deadline to contribute is the tax-filing deadline. This is typically April 15. So, for example, you can contribute $6,000 to a Roth IRA on April 1, 2021, for the tax year of 2020.

WHAT'S THE DEAL WITH TAXES?

You can contribute to an IRA with either pretax dollars or after-tax dollars, depending on the type.

A traditional IRA is also known as a pretax IRA. The amount you contribute to your traditional IRA will be deducted from that year's income tax. You are deferring your payment of taxes to a later date. In the future, you pay income tax on the total amount you withdraw. This means you end up paying taxes in the future on both your contributions and your growth. Simply put, avoid taxes today; pay taxes in the future.

A Roth, aka after-tax, IRA doesn't reduce your income tax today, but you don't pay taxes on your withdrawals when you retire. Simply put, you pay tax today but no tax in the future. Your withdrawals are tax-free, and the growth you receive in this account also avoids taxes.

There are many debates around which is better. Should you pay the taxes now or later? It's difficult to say. If you're not in a high tax bracket now, it could be a great time to take advantage of a Roth. On the other hand, if you could really use a tax break now, a pretax account could be great. If you won't touch this money for 30 or more years, a Roth IRA could be a good option to consider since you won't pay taxes on the growth. Because we don't know what tax rates will be in the future or the growth of your investments, it's difficult to have a clear-cut answer. Explore a few scenarios, and then trust your gut on this one. You can always do a little of both. The point here is to just do something for your future self.

WHEN CAN I TAKE THE MONEY OUT?

I am going to explain the most common, general rules. There

are exceptions to these, which I will not be covering. You can research these exceptions on the IRS's website, or ask a tax advisor for more information.

You can withdraw money from a traditional IRA at age 59 and a half. You pay income tax on the total amount withdrawn. If you withdraw money before that age, you pay a 10% penalty in addition to the taxes you owe on the withdrawal.

The rules today state that at age 72, you must begin to take withdrawals. This is called the minimum required distribution. I'm not going to get into details since this is not happening any time soon.

You can withdraw your contributions from a Roth IRA penalty-free at any time. This comes with tax paperwork, though. If you withdraw any *earnings* (money made in your account due to growth beyond the amount you've contributed) before age 59 and a half, you pay a 10% penalty in addition to extra income taxes. After that age, you can withdraw all money from your Roth IRA tax-free. There is no minimum required distribution rule.

HOW DO I INVEST IN THIS KIND OF PLAN?

You can open a traditional or Roth IRA at your bank or brokerage firm. This is like any other investment account. You can invest in all the same things we talked about in the past chapters—stocks, bonds, mutual funds, and so forth.

TRADITIONAL-TO-ROTH CONVERSION

You are always allowed to convert a traditional IRA to a Roth IRA. Why? Because the IRS would love for you to pay taxes now rather than defer them. It's money in their pocket today.

I already covered this briefly with the back-door contributions strategy, but what if you've already taken the tax benefits associated with a traditional IRA? How does the conversion work? You have to add the amount you convert to your income the year you do the conversion, and you pay taxes on it based on your income bracket.

Here's an example: You have a traditional IRA with $50,000. You leave your job to open a new business. This year, your income will be minimal. You are living off your savings. You decide to convert all $50,000 of your traditional IRA to a Roth IRA. Since you received a tax deduction in the past, you will get taxed on your $50,000 as income this year, which you are okay with since you'll be in a low tax bracket this year. Let's say the $50,000 grows to $120,000 by the time you are age 60. You withdraw $100,000 to buy a painting. Yes, you're a baller now. Guess what? You don't pay any taxes on the $100,000.

Most people don't want to voluntarily pay more taxes, but this could be a good choice if you experience a year or two of low income.

EMPLOYER RETIREMENT SAVINGS PLANS

If you are currently employed by a company and they offer a retirement plan, this may be the first place you look to save. These plans come in many different forms, but these are the most common:

- 401(k), which is typically used by corporations
- 403(b), which is usually offered by hospitals and schools
- 457(b), which is usually offered to local and state employees
- Thrift Savings Plan (TSP), which is available to federal government employees

Your employer may offer pretax and after-tax (Roth) options of these plans. This is similar to what we just reviewed with a traditional IRA and Roth IRA. If you're unclear about what your employer offers, just ask.

Although these plans have different names, many of the features and benefits are similar. They all have one goal in mind: to help you maintain your lifestyle once you retire. Many of these employer plans offer a matching component. You put money in, and your company will match your contribution up to a certain percentage of the salary. That's the minimum you should contribute. Everything your company contributes is free money for you, so why wouldn't you take advantage? Don't stop there. If your company will match 3%, that's awesome. You still are working toward contributing 15%. Don't settle for 3%. Let's talk details.

HOW MUCH CAN I CONTRIBUTE?

For all four types of employer retirement plans—401(k), 403(b), 457(b), and TSP—including their Roth options, if available, the maximum contribution is $19,500 in 2020 if you're under age 50.

Similar to the IRA rules, you can't contribute the maximum to both a pretax and its Roth counterpart. You can put money in each type of account, but your combined contributions cannot be more than that year's maximum, $19,500 in this example.

The contribution deadline is the last day of the calendar year, December 31.

BASED ON MY INCOME, AM I ALLOWED TO CONTRIBUTE?

Yes! There's no limit on your income when making contributions to an employer's retirement plan. You don't have to look at charts or call your tax advisor. If your employer offers it, you can contribute. Yay! Easy!

WHAT'S THE DEAL WITH TAXES?

The same rules that apply to IRAs apply to employer retirement plans. In a pretax plan, such as a traditional 401(k), your contributions reduce the amount of income tax you pay that year. You save money on taxes now. Woo-hoo! You pay income tax on your withdrawals when you retire. Darn! You are deferring taxes.

If you contribute to an after-tax plan, such as a Roth 401(k), your contributions do not reduce your income taxes that year. Boo. But you don't pay taxes when you withdraw money, and all your earnings are tax-free. Woo-hoo!

For example, let's say you earn $100,000 this year. You contribute $15,000 to your employer's retirement plan. At age 60, you withdraw $30,000.

If it's a pretax 401(k):

> Your total taxable income this year is $85,000.

> At age 60, you pay income tax on the full $30,000.

If it's a Roth 401(k):

> Your total taxable income this year is $100,000.

At age 60, you pay $0 in taxes on the $30,000.

WHEN CAN I TAKE THE MONEY OUT?

I am going to explain the most common, general rules as if you are actively working for the employer providing the plan. There are exceptions and additional rules if you don't work for them anymore. I will not be covering the majority of those rules. Many of these exceptions are specific to your employer. Contact your employer's plan administrator for the exact rules.

For both traditional 401(k)s and Roth 401(k)s, you can withdraw money at age 59 and a half. You have to qualify for a hardship withdrawal to access your money before that age. This option is subject to your plan, and additional penalties may apply.

You may have the ability to borrow money against your plan. Your ability to take a loan depends on your plan rules. You can typically borrow 50% of your account balance or $50,000, whichever is less. For example, if you have a balance of $20,000, you may be able to borrow $10,000. If your balance is $200,000, the most you can borrow is $50,000.

HOW DO I INVEST IN THIS KIND OF PLAN?

For an employer plan, your investment options will be provided to you. If you have questions, you can call your human resources (HR) department or the plan administrator to get a complete understanding of your options. This is great information to have before making your selections.

Okay, time for an emotional check-in. How are you feeling? Take a deep breath. Seriously, do it with me. I need to take one as I write this. There are ton of rules, strategies, and what-if scenarios that can get my mind spinning. This is the tip of the iceberg with retirement. I love geeking out on this stuff. It's normal to feel overwhelmed. Remember, you don't need to be an expert. I'm going to dive into one more option for entrepreneurs. If that's not you, you can skip to the next section.

SIMPLIFIED EMPLOYEE PENSION (SEP IRA)

A SEP IRA stands for simplified employee pension. It is a simple, tax-deferred retirement plan for anyone who is self-employed, owns a business, employs others, or earns freelance income. This isn't a business book, so I'm going to breeze over this area. My goal is to provide highlights. If they pique your interest, you can bring this to your tax advisor for more details.

EMPLOYER CONTRIBUTION LIMITS

This can be a bit confusing because you are the employer. Working with your tax advisor can help here. The employer can contribute 25% of the employee's total compensation or a maximum of $57,000 for the 2020 tax year, whichever is less.

If you're self-employed, your contributions are generally limited to 20% of your net income with a compensation limit of $285,000 for 2020.

The plan contributions are deductible for the business. Yay! Contributions aren't required every year. Double yay! This is a flexible plan. Business owners can experience a hiccup when they have employees, though: contribution percentages must be the same for employers and employees. This can be used to attract or maintain talent since it's a perk, but you need to financially plan that you can afford to make contributions for the whole team.

EMPLOYEE CONTRIBUTION LIMITS

You can also make contributions as an employee. The rules are the same as the traditional IRA. You can contribute a maximum of $6,000 if you're under age 50 for the 2020 tax year. If you do this as an employee, this counts against any other IRA as well. The $6,000 maximum contribution is the total contribution allowed by the IRS that employees can make to all their IRAs. This includes any SEP, traditional, or Roth contributions each year.

WHAT'S THE DEAL WITH TAXES?

The same rules that apply to a traditional (pretax) IRA apply to a SEP IRA.

WHEN CAN I TAKE THE MONEY OUT?

The same rules that apply to a traditional (pretax) IRA apply to a SEP IRA. There are some exceptions since this is an employer plan. You can speak with your tax advisor for more details.

HOW DO I INVEST IN THIS KIND OF PLAN?

You can open a SEP IRA at your bank or brokerage firm. This is like any other investment account. You can invest in all the same things we talked about in past chapters—stocks, bonds, mutual funds, and so forth.

RETIREMENT INVESTING IN ACTION

Let's check out some real-life examples from our main characters.

JESSICA'S ROCKIN' RETIREMENT

Jessica is filing taxes as single, works for a big company, doesn't own a home, and is a high-income earner. Based on her circumstances, she doesn't have many tax deductions. At age 35, it's difficult for her to know what her income will be in 10 years. It's even harder to predict what her income will look like when she's age 65. She thinks she'll move out of New York City eventually. Her dad keeps telling her a Roth IRA is the better option since she's avoiding future taxes on her growth, but she wants to save on the taxes she's paying right now.

Ideally, Jessica would like to participate in both a pretax and after-tax IRA. Jessica also has a few small 401(k)s outstanding from previous jobs. She's embarrassed that she doesn't know their amounts or where they're being held. Her homework is to track down these statements. She needs to know her balances, how she's invested, account numbers, and so forth in order to figure out next steps. Her initial thought is that since they're small amounts, she should cash them out.

Jessica does some research and discovers her company offers a Roth 401(k) option. It wasn't around when she first joined the company. She vaguely remembers getting emails about it a couple of years ago. She likes the idea of saving on taxes now, but she also likes the idea of not paying taxes in the future. She can afford to pay the taxes now. She wants to have flexibility in the future. She can't decide. Jessica opts to take advantage of both the Roth 401(k) and the traditional 401(k) her company offers.

For Jessica to max out her 401(k) plan, she needs to contribute about 13% of her income. She decides to split that between the pretax and post-tax 401(k) options, putting 7% in her pretax 401(k) and 6% in her post-tax Roth 401(k). Her employer does match 5% of her contributions. Their match will go directly into her pretax 401(k) since she is not paying taxes on their contributions this year. The only thing that will ever be in her Roth 401(k) is her personal contributions. She decides to stick with the life-cycle (or target-date) fund option her employer made available. It is the automatic default investment option based on her age. The asset allocation, underlying investments, and expense ratio look great to her. She believes this is the best option for her right now and isn't making any changes.

Jessica also does some research on what to do with her previous 401(k) plans. Her options are as follows:

1. Cash Out—This option is considered an early withdrawal. She will have to pay the 10% penalty plus the income taxes on the total amount. In total, she will lose about 40% of the balance to taxes and penalties. She quickly decides against this option.
2. Direct Rollover into a Pretax IRA—Jessica doesn't want to do this because she would need to open a new IRA. She already lost track of these accounts and wants to keep it simple. She decides against this option.
3. Direct Rollover into Her Existing Pretax 401(k)—Under her employer plan's rules, she is allowed to roll pretax money into her pretax 401(k). By doing this, Jessica is limiting her investment options; however, that is not Jessica's priority. She wants to keep things simple and likes the fund options available to her inside her company's 401(k).

Jessica chooses option 3. She decides to directly roll her previous

401(k)s into her current 401(k) simply due to convenience. Jessica moved from being overwhelmed by this financial stuff to being excited. She can make sense of it all. Putting it into practice is building her confidence. She knows how to ask questions. She can interpret answers that she found confusing in the past. Jessica thinks this isn't difficult; she just didn't know how to get started before.

ASHLEY'S RELAXATION RETIREMENT

Although Ashley is living with her fiancé, she is considered single when filing her taxes. We know she is focusing on saving for retirement. Ashley wants to bite the tax bullet now. She doesn't want to worry about paying taxes in the future. She wants to know if she has $100,000 in her account, she can withdraw $100,000. Having security in retirement is so important to her. She wants to eliminate extra variables. This gives her peace of mind.

Ashley confirms her employer does not offer a Roth 401(k) option, so she opens her own Roth IRA. Her pretax 401(k) at work offers 3% matching. She is going to contribute 3% to her 401(k). She is also going to max out her Roth IRA. She calculates how much she needs to contribute each month to hit the max by the end of the year, and she sets up automatic monthly contributions. After six months, she will increase her 401(k) contributions. She wants to pump up her retirement contributions, but she also wants to be realistic. She doesn't want to start contributing too much too fast and not be able to save for other goals.

MIKE AND SARAH'S RETIREMENT IN STYLE

Mike and Sarah haven't been focused on saving for retirement, not because they don't care. His primary goal is to grow his company.

Mike's company is growing fast, and he is running it alone. He doesn't have anybody helping him understand retirement savings strategies. They have been relying on Sarah's company's plan. They are now ready to explore more options. Sarah has been putting money away for her retirement. She is unclear if she's doing enough. They don't have strong opinions about which type of retirement account to use. They consider themselves a clean slate. They are excited to do more than what they've been doing.

Mike works with his CPA to set up a SEP IRA. For the next 5 years, Mike is going to focus on building up his retirement savings. Mike carves out a portion of his profits to reinvest in the company. He sets aside a portion of that reinvestment toward his SEP IRA. Although he knows this may temporarily slow the growth of the company, he is investing in his retirement. That gives him peace of mind.

As a couple, Mike and Sarah don't qualify for a Roth IRA. Their combined income is over the allowable limit. Sarah does have a Roth 401(k) option at work. She is going to start contributing 5%, but she wants to be able to contribute 15% in the future. She is intimidated by this since she is putting more toward her student loan debt every month. She is starting to doubt whether she can do all of this. This sets off a light bulb that she needs to circle back to her initial money mindset work. She acknowledges the thought, reframes her thinking, and moves through it. Logically, Sarah understands what she's doing. She understands her why. But this is a big change. Rather than looking at the big picture, she decides to focus on the now. In Sarah's mind, saving 5% now is doable. She doesn't need to stress out right now about how she'll get to 15% in the future. One step at a time.

JOURNAL EXERCISE

Now it's your turn! Here's an exercise to get you started in your retirement planning.

Step 1—Choose which type of retirement account you want to use.

Explore what you have available through your employer or on your own. What kind of account are you currently using? After exploring the options, what type of account do you want to use going forward? Why?

Step 2—Determine how much you can contribute.

If you are receiving a match from your employer, contribute at least the matching amount. That is a no-brainer.

If you're under the 15% Empowered Planning Golden Rule, create a goal to get you there. (I'll give you specifics for how to do this in the next chapter.)

Step 3—Get invested.

Invest the money you're contributing. Don't assume your contributions are getting invested. The default option may be cash (often in the form of a money market fund). You want to take advantage of the tax deferral in these accounts. Don't forget to participate in the market. Make sure your investments are in line with your time frame, risk tolerance, and current financial situation.

KEY TAKEAWAYS

In this chapter, we learned retirement today looks different than it did in the past. We still have Social Security, but it's not a huge amount of money, and pensions are not as common as they used to be. So what you save today will be your main source of income when you retire.

To know whether you've saved enough for retirement, you can use these rough savings goals by age:

- At age 30, you should have one times your salary in retirement savings.
- At age 40, you should have three times your salary in retirement savings.
- At age 50, you should have six times your salary in retirement savings.
- At age 60, you should have eight times your salary in retirement savings.
- At age 67, you should have ten times your salary in retirement savings.

Remember the Empowered Planning Golden Rule: Save a minimum of 15% of your gross income toward retirement.

There are many different types of retirement accounts. Explore the options available to you and select an option. No need to overthink this. Simply take action.

It's common to feel overwhelmed when planning for retirement. Let that be a lightbulb to do an emotional check-in. Acknowledge the thought, reframe your thinking, and move through it.

At this point, you know all the essentials and strategies you need to make investing your superpower. Congrats! All that's left is to put it all together. In the final phase of your Empower Plan, you'll learn how to take everything you've learned and really put it into action so you can make your dreams a reality.

Phase 3

Put It All Together

During this phase, you will:

- Explore the adjustable elements of financial goal planning to tailor your strategy so you can achieve your goals.
- Learn how to tie all the pieces together and make money moves like a *BOSS!*
- Explore how to choose an investment firm to partner with.
- Learn how to set your savings and investments on autopilot.
- Learn how to pivot when life happens and you're knocked off track.
- Receive templates for how to review your investments and do regular check-ins so your plan doesn't fall apart over time.

CHAPTER 10

BRINGING YOUR GOALS TO LIFE

Blind dates are the worst. Well, at least the anticipation. You don't know what to expect. You mentally prepare for a host of possibilities. My first blind date was with my friend's coworker. She and her hubby agreed, "He seems nice." Nice is one of those words that says a lot without saying anything at all. I was thinking bore-a-fill; yes, that's a Billy Madison reference. Since I was trying to get back out there, as they say, this seemed like an easy transition onto the dating scene. As I was getting ready for my date with Nice Guy, doubt started to creep in, which exploded into a full-on freak-out. I thought, "Why am I even doing this? Am I overflowing with desperation? What if he hasn't had a girlfriend in 10 years? What if he's amazing, and the world's messiest eater, me, grosses him out?"

Fast forward through that rabbit hole of nonsense. I'm sitting across the dinner table from Nice Guy at a new swanky restaurant. My palms are sweaty. I'm convinced he thinks I have a mouth twitch because of my awkward smiling. As the night progresses, it turns out he is actually a nice guy.

Even though Nice Guy wasn't "The One" and we didn't end up living happily ever after, the experience helped me grow. I worked through a fear and started to enjoy the dating journey. I let go of the need to be in control all the time. This is a consistent balancing act for me. I became willing to go with the flow, doors opened, my confidence grew, and I became clear about what I wanted from a partner and myself.

The momentum fear can build in our heads is often more dramatic than what we actually experience when we try. In Steven Pressfield's book *Do the Work*, he says, "Start before you're ready. Don't prepare. Begin." It's that simple. Begin. We all have competing priorities. Sulky Suzie is known to burst onto the scene as we plan financial goals. This time around, you know what to do. Acknowledge the thought, reframe your thinking, and move through it.

In Chapter 3, you explored what you wanted from life. You organized your goals into buckets by their time frames. It's time to turn those dreams into reality! When I take women through goal setting in Empowered Academy, the initial theme is overwhelm. This is totally normal. But as they work the steps, the clouds begin to lift, and this incredible shift happens. Women move from confusion and uncertainty to unwavering clarity and focus. Effective goal setting will change your life.

After working with thousands of people over the years, I've learned there's one main reason we miss the financial goals we set. Can you guess it? Ambiguity. Even though our intentions are good, when we make lofty, undescriptive goals, we set ourselves up for failure. Without targets and a finish line that keeps moving, staying motivated is challenging. The old belief that we must work harder to get what we want isn't the whole truth. In this chapter,

I'll introduce you to the concept of SMART goals, showing you how to create more-effective goals. I'll also lay out the different ways you can adapt and pivot when necessary so you can turn your dreams into reality. Let's get to it!

WORK SMARTER, NOT HARDER

SMART is an acronym for specific, measurable, achievable, relevant, and timely. It's an effective way to actually reach your goals and my go-to. I love this technique because it works. When I try to wing it, I easily get off track. I lose steam when I don't see results. Creating SMART goals gives you clear direction, emphasizes your priorities, and keeps you motivated. Yes to all of that, right? Here's the breakdown.

SPECIFIC—WELL-DEFINED, CLEAR GOALS

Being vague is the biggest goal killer. As you think about your goals, you want to drill down into every detail to remove guesswork. If your goal is to "save more money for retirement," elaborate on that. What is "more" money to you? If your goal is to "spend less money," does that mean you want to cut back on dining out? Or does it mean you want to spend less money shopping in the black hole of Amazon Prime? Define your financial goals in clear, simple terms.

MEASURABLE—CRITERIA USED TO IDENTIFY YOUR PROGRESS

How will you track your progress? This part should not feel like a chore. If you want to save money for a new business venture, then have a reminder once a month to see if you can increase your savings. If that feels like too much, make it every other month.

Tailor how you will measure your progress to your personality but keep yourself honest. You want to measure your progress in a way that keeps your goal top of mind and allows you to change course if you get off track.

ACHIEVABLE—REALISTIC AND WITHIN YOUR FINANCIAL MEANS TO ATTAIN

Shame and disappointment often come hand in hand when you miss goals you set for yourself. Set yourself up for success. Based on the resources you have available, is it realistic to achieve your goals? For most of us, having a savings goal of $100,000 in six months isn't realistic. Give yourself a break and keep it real. You don't want to give Sulky Suzie a reason to stop by if you could have prevented it.

RELEVANT—IMPORTANT AND PURPOSEFUL TO YOUR LIFE

Remember the Three Why Test in Chapter 3? Pull out those answers. Creating meaningful goals will inspire you to stick with them. What would happen if you were able to hit your financial goals? Visualize the outcome. When your goals are purposeful to your life, you are willing to make habitual changes. You stay motivated because you're emotionally attached to the end result. For example, being able to support my children through college is a way for me to honor my parents' struggle as immigrants in the United States. That won't get lost on me along the way. Know your why behind your goal and you will achieve it.

TIMELY—TAKE THE QUICK WINS

It's 3:00 a.m., you have a newborn baby keeping you company, you can't remember the last time you slept, but you get immediate satisfaction typing away on your phone. Click, swipe, done. A variety of baby swaddles with next-day delivery are on their way. As a society, we are overly familiar with instant gratification. Thanks, Amazon. Since you can't buy your dream home or retirement on Prime, saving for your financial goals can lose its luster over time.

The solution? Break down your goals into bite-size pieces. Celebrate the quick wins along the way.

For example, on my Say No to Mom Jeans journey, knowing I wanted to lose weight would catapult me into anxiety. I shifted my focus to exercising four times per week to increase my energy levels. Celebrating the small wins generated momentum toward the bigger weight-loss goal.

Create actionable goals that you can achieve quickly and celebrate your wins. Check out the Empower Wins Worksheet in the digital assets.

SMART IN ACTION

Now that you're familiar with the SMART goal concept, let's take a look at an example. If your goal is to save more for retirement, that's too vague; make it SMART:

> "On March 1, I will increase the automatic contributions to my 401(k) by 1%. Every month, I will check to see if I can increase my contributions by 1%. I will hit my retirement savings goal of 5% by August 30."

This goal meets our SMART criteria. Setting a date of March 1 to increase contributions by 1% is specific. It's measurable since I'll be checking each month. It's achievable since saving 1% is within my budget to afford each month. The goal is relevant because I am trying to max out my 401(k) to take full advantage of its tax savings and tax deferral. Finally, reaching my goal by August 30 makes this goal timely. Instead of waiting for 30 years to get a win, I get a win in six months. Saving for retirement that's 30 years away is not motivating. Making a concerted effort to increase your retirement savings over the next six months is achievable. Do it. Celebrate the win! Creating a realistic action plan will keep you motivated and focused on the end goal.

UNDERSTAND THE NUMBERS BEHIND YOUR GOAL

In Phase 1 of your Empower Plan, you created goals in theory, but they probably weren't very specific and you likely had no tangible way to measure your ability to succeed. As a result, it would be easy to fall short of these goals and brush off failures because *insert shoulder shrug* they weren't achievable in the first place. How do you fix this? To create SMART goals, you need to understand the numbers behind your goal. Don't worry, you don't need to be good at math. That's why we have calculators.

I'll walk you through this step by step using Jessica as an example to illustrate how this works. In this example, Jessica already has an established emergency fund. Remember, this is a necessity and shouldn't be overlooked. I won't be going over a detailed example of this in the interest of time, but if you don't already have one established, create a SMART goal to make it happen.

Now let's dive in.

JESSICA'S HOME SWEET HOME BUCKET

In Chapter 3, we learned Jessica wants to have a down payment for her first home. Her desired time frame is 7 years. Jessica doesn't have a strategy for getting there. Here is the process:

Step 1: Using real estate apps, check out the average home sales price in your ideal location.

Step 2: Run mortgage payment estimates to see what's realistic to spend on housing each month.

When considering your monthly payment, keep in mind the Empowered Planning Golden Rule: No more than 28% of your gross income should go toward your monthly housing payment, including principal, interest, taxes, and insurance. Use an online calculator if you don't know these numbers yet.

Step 3: Determine the down payment.

> **Empowered Planning Golden Rule:** Put down 20% of the total value of the home as a down payment.

If you put less than 20% down toward a home, you are subject to pay private mortgage insurance, which increases your monthly payment. Private mortgage insurance typically falls off after 5 years, with some exceptions. Here is where the fun begins and the magic happens.

After completing steps 1 and 2, Jessica discovers her ideal home cost is roughly $480,000. To have a down payment of at least 20% of the home's total value, she needs to have $96,000 ($480,000 × 0.2) in cash in 7 years.

Since Jessica has always lived in an apartment, she wants extra cash on hand to furnish the house. That adds an additional savings goal of $10,000.

Jessica has a savings account with money she's saved over the years. The main purpose of the money in this account hasn't been defined yet. She decides to dedicate $35,000 from this savings account to her Home Sweet Home bucket.

Okay, so Jessica wants to have $96,000, the 20% down payment, plus $10,000 for the extras. This makes a grand total of $106,000. She has $35,000 saved. She needs to make up the difference in 7 years. Jessica needs to save an additional, beep boop bop beep (yes, that's what a calculator sounds like), $71,000.

In order for Jessica to meet her goal in 7 years, she would need to save about $10,143 per year or $845 per month. Jessica doesn't think it's realistic to maintain a savings of $845 per month for 7 years. She has competing priorities such as annual vacations, a potential wedding, a new car, and retirement. So now what? Should she throw in the towel? Heck no! It's time to examine the adjustable elements of goal setting to discover the best path to take.

FOUR ADJUSTABLE ELEMENTS OF FINANCIAL GOAL SETTING

Life is not linear. Even when everything looks good on paper, you may need to adjust along the way. Your goals aren't achieved in theory. They're real, just like you. You need an Empower Plan that can roll with the punches. I'm going to teach you how to use the adjustable elements of your goals so you are set up for success. That way, when life happens and you need to make changes down the road, you have an easy process to follow.

I've broken down the adjustable elements of financial goal setting into four options:

Option 1: Adjust the dollar amount of your goal.

Option 2: Adjust the time frame of your goal.

Option 3: Adjust the periodic contributions to your goal.

Option 4: Adjust your investments.

Let's circle back to Jessica's Home Sweet Home bucket to see how this works.

OPTION 1: ADJUST THE DOLLAR AMOUNT OF YOUR GOAL

The basis of Jessica's Home Sweet Home bucket is the total dollar amount. Does Jessica want to change that? She explores buying a home that's less than $480,000. After some research, Jessica isn't finding appealing options in the lower price range. She explores alternative locations, but this puts her forty-five minutes away from her job and friends. She begins to get discouraged. Jessica decides to stick with her original goal of $480,000.

OPTION 2: ADJUST THE TIME FRAME OF YOUR GOAL

Jessica is open to pushing out the time frame past 7 years. She runs the numbers on saving $400 per month instead of $845 per month. In this scenario, it will take her close to 15 years to save $71,000.

Jessica is okay pushing her time frame out a little bit, but she doesn't want to push it out to 15 years, so she continues looking at her other options.

OPTION 3: ADJUST THE PERIODIC CONTRIBUTIONS TO YOUR GOAL

Jessica's ideal monthly contribution is $400 per month. She can save the $845 per month required to meet her goal in 7 years, but she's not thrilled about this option. By doing so, she'll have to tighten her belt on her monthly spending. Before she resigns herself to this monthly payment, she looks at her final option.

OPTION 4: ADJUST YOUR INVESTMENTS—USE YOUR SUPERPOWER

Simply contributing money each month to your financial goals will get you only so far. You can use this option to adjust the potential growth rate of your investments. At $400 per month, it will take Jessica close to 15 years to save $71,000 by simply sitting in cash. Let's say Jessica instead invests her initial contribution of $35,000 plus $400 per month. Using an average growth rate of 6%, she'll end up with $95,000 at the end of 7 years (I'll explain more on calculating growth rates in just a moment). Although she's still $11,000 short of her goal, this beats having her money sit in cash by a long shot.

Those are your four options, the adjustable elements you can play with when creating your financial goals. This is all about *your* preferences. For example, let's say you commit to cutting your dining out by half so each month you have extra money to throw toward your goals. The result is you reaching your goal 2 years faster. That's powerful information to know. You will feel less like you're on a budget and more like you're on the fast track to making your dreams come true. The opposite is also true. You may decide that ordering takeout helps you maintain balance in your hectic life. Reaching your goals 2 years faster sounds great, but you will be stressed and burned out on your way there. No, thank you, right? There's no right answer. You choose the options that best suit your current lifestyle and personality. You're in the driver's seat. You get to make that call.

GROWTH CALCULATIONS

So how did I figure out all those numbers? I didn't pull them out of thin air; I got them by plugging Jessica's initial investment, monthly contribution, growth rate, and time frame into a financial calculator. If you know your way around an HP 10BII, you can do this yourself. If you aren't into pocket protectors, you can use an online growth calculator. Different websites offer this for free. For instance, Nerdwallet.com has one under the name Investment Return Calculator, and Bankrate.com offers one under the name Investment Calculator. Check out the digital assets for the most up-to-date URLs.

Running growth rates through an investment growth calculator will help you toggle between your four options and customize your goal strategy to fit your lifestyle.

As you begin investing, you'll get an idea of your realistic growth rates and the hypothetical growth rates possible with some changes to your investing. For now, to simplify this process, here are some hypothetical, realistic growth rates based on the time frames of your goals (if you're conservative by nature, use a growth rate on the lower end of the ranges listed):

- Goal within 0 to 3 years

- Assume a 0% growth rate or use the current interest rate you're earning in your savings account (or whatever cash-like instrument you're using). You know you need this money in the short term or have it on the side for emergencies, so what's the point in taking risk by investing it more aggressively?
- Goal within 3 to 5 years
  - Assume a 3% to 5% growth rate.
- Goal within 5 to 10 years
  - Assume a 5% to 7% growth rate.
- Goal within 10 or more years
  - Assume an 8% to 9% growth rate.

Back to Jessica. By simply saving toward her Home Sweet Home bucket of $106,000, she was going to have to dedicate $845 per month for 7 years to make up the gap of $71,000 (the $106,000 total minus her $35,000 already saved).

Let's review her four options again.

Option 1: Adjust the dollar amount of your goal.

What if Jessica lowers her goal total from $106,000? Jessica decides not to lower her goal because it would mean living forty-five minutes away from her ideal location.

Option 2: Adjust the time frame of your goal.

What if Jessica extends her time frame from 7 years to 8 years? Jessica's initial investment is $35,000. She contributes $400 per month toward this bucket. Using the average annual growth rate of 6%, after 8 years, Jessica's total balance is $106,000. Woo-hoo!

Option 3: Adjust the periodic contributions to your goal.

Here, we stick with the average growth rate of 6% on her investment. Jessica's initial investment is $35,000. She contributes $500 per month instead of $400 per month. Using the average growth rate of 6%, after 7 years, Jessica will have about $105,000 saved. Woo-hoo!

Option 4: Adjust your investments.

What if Jessica changes her investments? This is an option, but considering a higher-risk investment may not be worth the potential downside.

What does Jessica decide to do? She falls somewhere between option 2 and option 3. Jessica decides that she wants to increase her monthly contributions to $500 per month *and* extend her time frame to 8 years for cushion room. If she can hit her goal before 8 years, she will be thrilled. If it takes her the full 8 years, she won't be disappointed. She's excited to save for her goal. She also wants to enjoy her day-to-day lifestyle without too many compromises. We'll look at how Jessica makes her goal SMART later in this chapter.

PIVOTING AND PRIORITIZING

Creating realistic, achievable financial goals is not a one-time task. You need concrete numbers to see if your goals are realistic. But this exercise is alive, not stagnant. It's just like the Greek philosopher Heraclitus said, "The only constant in life is change." The process of creating the lifestyle you want must be fluid and flexible. Throughout this journey, you will experience both pleasant surprises and unanticipated roadblocks. Your priorities will shift over time. You are in the driver's seat, and your ability to pivot your plan is crucial to your success.

Let's continue on with the example of Jessica's Home Sweet Home bucket. Based on the assumptions we ran, she has the potential to achieve her goal in year 8 or even year 6 if her investments perform better than expected. We don't know if home values and interest rates will be higher, lower, or similar in 6 to 8 years. Jessica is also on pace to be earning a higher income in the near future. What if she can start contributing more each month? What if Jessica gets married and her goals shift? None of that is important today. Jessica can pivot and adapt her money goals as her situation changes. What's important right now is she creates an actionable guide to building wealth. When you're creating your SMART financial goals, please read this in your mother's voice: "Do your best."

Let's look at another example so you get more familiar with how you can apply this to your situation.

ASHLEY'S RELAXATION RETIREMENT BUCKET

Currently, as discussed in the previous chapter, Ashley's contributing 3% to her 401(k) account. She is receiving a 3% match from her company. Her existing balance in her 401(k) is $25,000. She is interested in maxing out her Roth IRA and increasing her contributions to her 401(k) to 6% within the next 3 years.

After reviewing her Lifestyle Guide, she eliminated unnecessary expenses and felt a weight lift off her shoulders. She can significantly increase her monthly contributions. Ashley can reach her goal of maxing out her Roth IRA, *but*—and I mean this with a big "but"; no, not your friend Lisa with the big booty, stay focused—if she wants to increase her 401(k) contributions, she is taking money away from her other goals. She examines her goals, her whys behind them, and reviews the four different adjustable options.

So what does Ashley do? Even though she wants to buy a home and own her own business, retirement is her priority. She prefers to push out the time frames on her other goals to focus on saving for retirement now. Ashley is not abandoning her other goals in pursuit of retirement. That's not the purpose of your Empower Plan. She's simply prioritizing and adjusting some of her goals' timelines so she can have it all.

There's no right answer; whatever you decide to do is unique to you. Another person in Ashley's scenario may choose to focus on starting their business. When you are clear on your goals, prioritization comes authentically. You begin to build unwavering motivation and momentum behind your Empower Plan. It's no longer about money as a material thing but about your lifestyle, your pursuit of happiness.

BALANCING YOUR GOALS

As you work through your goals, balancing them is part of the bigger picture. Ideally, you should calculate your desired scenario for each goal. Once you can see them all, go back and adjust them to make them work using the adjustable elements we talked about earlier. You may find you want to eliminate some goals or that new ones pop up. Let's take a look at another example of how to balance your goals.

MIKE AND SARAH'S HEY HEY VACAY BUCKET

Mike and Sarah's short-term goal is to take one big annual trip and smaller weekend getaways if possible. They aren't sure if this is realistic. They haven't kept a close eye on their spending in the past. Sarah thinks they need around $5,000 to $7,000. Mike strongly disagrees. He believes they spend a lot more and doubts they can juggle it all financially. They start by figuring out the numbers behind their goal.

Step 1—Review their previous spending.

How much do they typically spend on their big trips, and how much do their smaller getaways run them?

They looked at their previous 2 years since this information is easy to access. On average, they spent $15,000 each year on trips, which caught Sarah off guard. Sarah was feeling irresponsible and guilty that she had over $100,000 of student loan debt and was unaware of spending this much on trips. She was dumbfounded by it all. How could she be so seemingly smart and successful but so lost when it came to finances? If this happens to you, let it be a light bulb that Sulky Suzie wants to turn on the blinders and keep you down. But you have a plan: acknowledge it, reframe your thinking, and move through it. The idea of having to achieve financial success and pay off all your debt immediately is overwhelming to anyone. The solution for Sarah in this moment is to take baby steps. This whole exercise is raising her financial awareness. That's forward progress. She is now creating financial goals that are in line with her values. That's forward progress. She has a partner who is ready to take this on together. That's amazing. Sarah emotionally bounces back the following week. She's able to digest the numbers, the whys behind her goals, and get planning.

Step 2—Create a separate bucket dedicated to their vacations and getaways.

Mike and Sarah have a large checking account with no goals attached. As trips come up, they see a pile of cash in their account and quickly lose track of how much they spend. Creating a separate Vacation bucket creates transparency and a preestablished budget. When they buy plane tickets or book hotels, the money comes directly out of the Vacation bucket. This money is not invested. Since they will use it in the next year or two, it needs to be safe and liquid.

Step 3—Assign a dollar amount to this goal and stick to it.

After running the numbers on travel costs, hotel stays, and dining while on vacation, Mike and Sarah decide they want to dedicate $15,000 to vacations and getaways every year, provided they can also make a bigger dent in Sarah's student loan debt. If not, they'll go back to the drawing board and decrease how much they dedicate toward this bucket. They currently have $3,000 saved toward their Hey Hey Vacay bucket. They each need to add $250 per paycheck, $500 per month, to meet their goal of $15,000.

MIKE AND SARAH'S BYE BYE DEBT BUCKET

In addition to a short-term goal related to vacations, Mike and Sarah have a long-term goal of paying off Sarah's student loan debt. Thinking about her loans causes instant overwhelm. Mike's constant stress about her debt causes tension between them on a regular basis. At this point, they both want to create a plan that focuses on tackling Sarah's student loan debt so they can sleep better at night. Here is the process they take.

Step 1—Understand the total goal amount.

They start by reviewing their Student Loan Debt Worksheet (available in the digital assets) and figure out the total debt balance: $100,000.

Step 2—Determine extra monthly contributions.

Sarah figures out the minimums for each of her student loans and then reviews her Lifestyle Guide to determine how much extra she can throw at her loans each month without sacrificing her other goals. Sarah looks at how much she's spending on self-care and is motivated to move a portion of that toward her student loans. She has a group of friends who do monthly spa treatments, but they tack on brunch and leisure shopping afterward. Sarah looks back at the last six months. She was shocked at how much she was spending in one day. She loves this one-on-one time with her girlfriends since her schedule is hectic. Instead of a whole spa treatment, she'll suggest mani/pedis every other month and skip the shopping afterward. Up until now, Sarah has been doing the ostrich thing, burying her head in the sand when it comes to money. She feels relief going through this exercise. Her biggest pain point is the overwhelm of having to climb this giant debt mountain. She didn't realize how much money she had available to throw at her student loans. Paying down her debt now seems realistic. She's pumped.

Step 3—Commit to a payoff strategy.

Sarah needs to find an accelerated payoff strategy that she can stick with to build momentum and confidence. Sarah refinanced her student loans a year ago. Here are the current terms:

Total balance is $100,000.

Interest rate is 6%.

Loan term is 15 years.

Monthly minimum payment is about $850.

If Sarah sticks to this schedule, after 15 years, she will have paid a total of $152,000. Seeing these numbers pushes Sarah's motivation into high gear. If she pays off the debt faster, she could save a lot of money on interest—up to $50,000. Mike and Sarah can use this extra savings toward a bigger home. Seeing this with financially aware eyes, Sarah decides now is the time to tackle this. Based on Sarah's Lifestyle Guide, she can put an extra $200 toward her loans each paycheck. Mike agrees to match Sarah's $200 each paycheck. Their combined total in extra payments is $800 per month.

Mike and Sarah can pay off $100,000 of student loan debt at the end of 6 years without compromising their other financial goals and save about $32,000 in interest payments. I'll say that again. Mike and Sarah can create a plan to pay off over $100,000 of debt in 6 years without giving up their lifestyle.

But they do need to make *some* compromises. By shifting their focus to paying down debt, Mike and Sarah are taking money away from another goal, such as saving more for a bigger home. They get to decide what they want to achieve and how quickly they want to get there.

In this example, it's important to note option 4 for adjusting the goal is not available. As they get paid, they are paying down debt. There is no time to invest the money. If you're looking at these numbers saying, "There's no way I could do that," that's Sulky Suzie. Maybe these aren't your numbers. The whole point of this exercise is to figure out what yours are so you can take action. You're on the path to empowerment. That starts internally.

There are many incredible side effects to increasing your financial awareness. Sarah, for instance, began talking about money with confidence, which spilled over into her career. She began to negotiate a pay raise and promotion with her company. Her proposal illustrated her initial job requirements versus her current responsibilities and her ambition to take on larger projects. Her employer created a six-month development program to keep them both on track. Sarah was granted a new title right away and will be given a pay raise at the end of the six-month development program.

MAKING YOUR GOALS SMART

It's time to bring this all together. By now, you know what you want, with the numbers to back it up. You're ready to make your goals SMART. Let's look at how our main characters do this.

JESSICA'S HOME SWEET HOME BUCKET

Jessica's house money goal: $106,000 in 8 years.

Jessica's SMART goal: On March 1, I will set up automatic contributions of $500 (achievable) on the fifteenth of each month (specific) to be directly deposited and automatically invested into a mutual fund in my investment account nicknamed Home Sweet Home. On September 1, I will check (measurable) to see if I can increase my contribution amount to make sure I can have my down payment in 8 years (relevant). By March of next year, I will have hit my one-year (timely) savings goal of $6,000 toward my Home Sweet Home bucket.

Jessica wants to push herself to increase her contributions if possible and also keep herself honest. If she begins to spend money in areas that aren't a priority, this six-month check-in will put her back on track. Jessica is using the following March as her goal to celebrate the quick win. Next March, she'll create a new SMART goal for her Home Sweet Home bucket. Make sense? Remember that building wealth doesn't happen by accident. Break down your larger goals. Take the quick win to build momentum. Saving and investing for your future isn't easy-peasy. You're the one making it all happen. Celebrate *you* along the way!

ASHLEY'S RELAXATION RETIREMENT BUCKET

Ashley's goal is to contribute the maximum amount allowable to her Roth IRA each year and increase her 401(k) contributions. Instead of saying, "I want to save more in my 401(k)," let's take a look at how to make this SMART.

Ashley's retirement savings goal: Max out her annual Roth IRA contributions at $6,000 by the end of this year and increase her 401(k) contributions to 6% by the end of 3 years from now.

Ashley's SMART goal: Starting on January 1, I'll directly contribute $500 each month (specific and achievable) from my checking account to my Roth IRA. I will check to see how comfortable I am with my month-to-month expenses on April 1 (measurable). I will hit my retirement (relevant) savings goal of $6,000 in my Roth IRA on December 1 (timely).

On June 1, I will increase my 401(k) contributions to 4% (specific and achievable). On December 1, I will see if I can increase my contributions by 1% or more (measurable). I will continue to do this every six months until I reach my 401(k) savings goal (relevant) of 6% per year in 3 years (timely).

MIKE AND SARAH'S HEY HEY VACAY BUCKET

Mike and Sarah's vacation money goal: $12,000 this year (their annual total is $15,000, but they already have $3,000 saved, so they need to save for the $12,000 difference).

Mike and Sarah's SMART goal: Starting on January 1, we will automatically contribute $250 (specific and achievable) each per paycheck (measurable) into our vacation account (relevant). We will hit our savings goal of $12,000 for vacations this year (timely).

MIKE AND SARAH'S BYE BYE DEBT BUCKET

Mike and Sarah's debt elimination goal: Pay off $100,000 of student loan debt in 6 years.

Mike and Sarah's SMART goal: Starting March 1, we will directly debit $800 a month, $200 each per paycheck (specific and achievable), from our joint checking account to pay down Sarah's student loans. On September 1 (measurable), we will check to see if we can afford to pay down (relevant) more. We will reach our annual payoff goal of $9,600 on March 1 of next year (timely).

JOURNAL EXERCISE

Now it's your turn! Here's a cheat sheet on how to do this; you can also refer to the digital assets for a down-loadable worksheet:

- Organize your goals into buckets by their time frames.
- Determine how much money you need to reach each of your goals.
- Determine your starting balance. How much do you already have saved toward each of these goals? Don't stress if it's zero; it's a fact—nothing more than that. If you start to feel bad about your balance, it's Sulky Suzie, and she's not invited to stay long.
- Figure out the dollar amount of your gap.
- Refer to your Lifestyle Guide and determine how much you can contribute to each goal per month.
- Use an investment calculator to run growth assumptions.
- Based on the numbers you see, pivot based on your preferences.
- Make your goals SMART.

You're setting up systems that encourage success, and with each success, you build momentum. The rest is history. I'm excited to see what you can create!

KEY TAKEAWAYS

In this chapter, we introduced the concept of the SMART acronym and how making your goals specific, measurable, achievable, relevant, and timely can impact your success rate. We also learned how to run an analysis of your financial goals, adjust different elements, and pivot when necessary. We tied it all together by showing real-life examples of how our main characters made their goals SMART.

As you begin to create your SMART financial goals, allow yourself some grace. If life happens and you need to adjust, modify your goals. Don't wing it. Stick to the formula even as you need to pivot. You want to set yourself up for success.

As you go through this, if Sulky Suzie starts showing up, whatever your fear or disappointment is, say it out loud. Call a friend and tell them. I promise, you will find a way to laugh and surrender to reality. You'll get what you want; you just can't swipe up, down, or right to get it in an instant. Boo, right? You'll get there. Just be SMART about it!

In the final chapter of the book, we're going to bring everything home and go through the action steps to start taking right now to make your Empower Plan a reality.

CHAPTER 11

MAKING MONEY MOVES

It's 2020 as I write this.

One hundred years ago, the 19th Amendment to the US Constitution passed, giving women in the United States the right to vote.

Fifty years ago, the Women's Strike for Equality took place. At 5:00 p.m. on 5th Street in New York City, thousands of women stood side by side, making it impossible for cars to pass. They stood together after a long day of work, in the dead heat of the summer, to fight for equality in the workforce. My favorite slogans from that day are "I Am Not a Barbie Doll" and "Storks Fly—Why Can't Mothers?"

Today...

Women are paid $0.81 for every $1.00 a man makes. The stats are even worse for minority women. This can reach up to a $900,000 income pay gap over a lifetime of earnings.

Today…

Men have account balances that are 50% larger than women.

Today…

Women are living longer than men.

Right now…

You need to take charge of your financial future. Be a loud voice in this movement. Lead by example.

No, things are not equal. But today, as a woman in America, *you* get to decide what kind of lifestyle you want now and for your future. The groundwork has been laid by thousands of women before us. Let's continue to honor that. Whatever obstacles you perceive may be in your way are just that. Your perception. You can change that. When it comes to creating and living the lifestyle you want, people don't plan to fail; they fail to plan. Not you. This is where we tie it all together and make you unstoppable.

This is where the real work starts. By now, you know what to do. You know why you should do it. In this chapter, we'll put it all together. You'll learn the step-by-step guide for implementing your Empower Plan. I've outlined five steps to make this simple. I'll finish off the chapter explaining what to do after everything is set up. The answer isn't nothing. Sorry! The tough work will be out of the way soon. The rest will be a piece of cake.

STEP 1—CONFIRM YOUR GOALS

It's time we let out a "Woo-hoo!" You're close to the finish line.

Let's drive this home. Before I walk you through how the magic happens, you need to revisit your goals. This will allow the steps to fall into place easily. This is not the time to put things on the back burner. You've been working toward this. You went to retirement boot camp. You always need to know your why. Otherwise, what's the point of what we're doing? Money? No. Money is temporary. What we are doing will change your life.

By now, your goals should be nicknamed into separate buckets. You can use the Investment Goal Strategy Worksheet available in the digital assets or whatever works for you. Keep it handy. You'll refer to it as you put the final touches on your Empower Plan. Use this as a template:

Goal Name:

Emergency Fund: Do NOT spend.

Goal Amount:

$15,000

What will this goal do for you?

Give me the peace of mind I haven't had in the past. It will give me flexibility in the event of an unplanned expense.

What is your desired target asset allocation?

Goal's time frame: Short-term time frame in case I have an emergency.

Tolerance to risk: I don't want to take any risk.

Current financial situation: Stable, but I don't have a cushion.

Desired asset allocation: 100% cash.

Why?

You always want to know your why behind the target asset mix you've chosen. This is particularly handy when you're working through changes to your situation.

I will need easy access to this money. My priority is to preserve my balance. I don't want to take any risk.

What is your investment strategy?

Money market fund in an investment account. This will be separate from my checking account. I don't want to be able to easily withdraw from this account.

What will your initial deposit be?

$3,000

What will you contribute biweekly or monthly?

Every two weeks, I will contribute $500.

What is your SMART goal?

Starting August 1, I will contribute $500 (specific and achievable) each paycheck to my emergency fund savings account. Every three months (measurable), I will check to see if I can increase my savings by $50. I'll reach my emergency fund savings goal (relevant) by August 1 next year (timely).

Reestablishing your goals will help you execute your plan simply and quickly. Without doing the work beforehand, you can get hung up on details. You end up treading water rather than making money moves. Now it's your turn; confirm all your goals.

STEP 2—CHOOSE AN INVESTMENT FIRM

This step is critical. Just as there are many investment options available, there are a variety of investment firms. What do you value most when partnering with an investment firm? Based on my own experiences and the most common criteria of my previous clients, there are four key factors to consider: value, product offering, service, and credibility.

VALUE

The first thing to consider is cost. I don't mean looking for the cheapest account or investment. Think of cost relative to value. Every company is going to make money one way or another. They may state the cost up front or build it into a product offering. Fees aren't bad, but they need to be relevant. There's a huge focus on cost in this industry. In the last 10 years, almost every investment firm has been able to lower their margins. They are providing better relationships to investors at a lower cost. This trend is great for us. Are there account maintenance fees? Are there investing minimums you need to meet? What features and benefits are available to you? Ask away. Find the best value for your money.

PRODUCT OFFERING

There are a handful of investment firms that have open architecture. This means they have unlimited offerings, such as thousands of mutual funds, ETFs, stocks, bonds, commodities, currencies, and more. This is important. You want a company that can grow with you. Your needs will be different in the future. As you adapt, you want your investment firm to provide support. So pay attention to the full range of their product offerings, even if you won't use it all right now.

SERVICE

Explore how the investment firm will support you once you become a client. Is their website user friendly? How about their app? What's their cybersecurity like? What sort of phone support do they offer? How knowledgeable are the people answering the phones? Can you get ahold of someone if you call? Do they offer local support? Ask away. Look for impartial reviews as well. There are many publications out there that do financial website reviews and publish the information in succinct formats.

CREDIBILITY

You also want to consider the firm's overall credibility. New isn't necessarily better when it comes to your personal financial security. By choosing a firm that has been well established for many years, you can feel more secure in your choice. After considering value, product offering, and service, I filtered for investment firms that have also been around for over a decade. Here are the three at the top of the list:

Charles Schwab
www.charlesschwab.com

Vanguard

https://investor.vanguard.com/home

Fidelity Investments

www.fidelity.com

Take a peek around. Play with the websites. Call their customer support. Check out their offerings. Choose a company you feel aligns with you and future you.

WORKING WITH A FINANCIAL ADVISOR OR FINANCIAL PLANNER

I want to mention that working with a financial advisor is valuable. As a financial advisor, I had access to many resources I could provide to my clients and I was consistently getting tasked with thinking outside the box and taking a holistic approach to creating financial plans. When you don't qualify to work with a professional or are facing high fees to gain access, you can do this yourself. When you start to have more than $300,000 to $400,000 to invest, I would open the door to a professional advisor. You want to make sure someone is watching your back, introducing new planning concepts, keeping you abreast of new tax changes, and bringing you resources or products you didn't have access to before. By doing the work you are now, you will build wealth. You'll be able to ask questions confidently and digest their answers. You'll build the knowledge base to have thoughtful discussions with a professional when they make recommendations. For now, continue down this path, but tackling your financial plan with a trusted partner should be part of the bigger picture.

STEP 3—OPEN YOUR ACCOUNTS

Carve out time to open your new investment accounts when you're not in a rush. You may run into little hiccups. You may need to pick up the phone and call a customer service rep to complete it correctly. Patience, my friend, patience. Once you open the account, give it a nickname; make it fun! Align your emotional drivers to your financial goals. This will keep your fire lit.

Open a separate account for each bucket. You don't want all your financial goals to be in one account. Your investment objectives will be different, giving each a unique asset allocation. Keep it simple for yourself.

Special Note: If you're establishing an employer-sponsored retirement plan, such as a 401(k), you can work with your HR group to set this up. Use the channels they have created. Select how much you want to contribute from each paycheck. Select your investments. Follow through to make sure it's done in a timely fashion. Set a reminder to check its success after a few pay cycles.

STEP 4—FUND YOUR ACCOUNTS

To fund your account and automate anything, you'll need to set up a link for the cash flow. Most people find a checking account link easiest. This provides greater control over increasing, decreasing, or pausing your contributions, but you can also do this directly through your paycheck. Decide what works best for you. If you're contributing to an employer-sponsored plan, such as a 401(k), those contributions come directly out of your paycheck.

Refer to your Investment Goal Strategy Worksheet.

Step 1: Transfer your initial investment into your new account.

Step 2: Purchase your chosen investment once the transfer is complete.

If you're starting the account with a small dollar amount, go ahead and make a one-time purchase. What if you're moving a large chunk of cash? Say you're moving over $50,000. It's been sitting in cash, so you are hesitant to buy $50,000 of "Fund HNH" in one shot. I get that. In this case, you can consider dollar cost averaging.

Dollar cost averaging is a strategy where you invest a fixed amount of money into the same investment at consistent intervals over time. For example, every month you invest $500 into the same fund over 5 years. Each month, you are purchasing the same dollar amount at varying prices. Over time, your cost per share will be an average of the fund's price.

In this case, you can set up an automatic investment plan for the $50,000. Divvy it up into equal investments over twelve months. In this example, on the first of every month, $4,000 will be invested into "Fund HNH" for twelve months. You can do this automatically or manually. Check out the features available and make a decision today. Don't leave anything undecided. Take action.

STEP 5—AUTOMATE

I am all for automation. Imagine being able to build wealth while it's out of sight, out of mind. Great, right? So automate and simplify.

By now, you have a specific investment strategy for each of your buckets. You can work with the investment firm you've selected if you need help selecting your investments. It's okay to not know everything. If you need help, ask. Let's say you've opened an account and know you want to buy "Fund HNH." Now you need to automatically contribute and simultaneously invest in this fund. Decide if you're going to do this biweekly or monthly.

Check out the details for how to set this up. Do you need to fund your account with an initial cash first? Do you need to own the fund already before automatic investing can be set up? Is there a minimum amount you need to meet? If it's not obvious to you on the website, pick up the phone. Find out the proper steps to make this happen.

If you're buying ETFs, individual stocks, or individual bonds, you'll need to do this manually each month. Find out the features available so you can automate as much as possible.

Automation is great in theory, but if you don't execute, what are we doing here? Make it happen. You got this!

That's it. Wooo-hoooo! or yay!—whichever one comes naturally to you. Seriously. You're amazing. Sit in this moment. Celebrate you. You're taking care of yourself. You're not waiting for someone to swoop down and do it for you. You are owning your power. I'm proud of you, girl!

MONITORING, REBALANCING, AND PIVOTING

The hardest part is done. Phew! Before you sail off into the sunset, I want to share tips on how to maintain your Empower Plan. Your life will change, and your plan will need to change alongside it. So it's important to continue monitoring, rebalancing, and pivoting your financial plan.

If you run into an unexpected change or life event, revisit your financial goals. Examples of these changes are an increase or decrease in pay, a marriage or divorce, a new addition to your family, things like that.

Revisit your financial buckets, your goals. Match up your time frame, your new financial situation, and your tolerance to risk. Based on those factors, you may want to update your asset allocation to accurately reflect your objectives. For example, you have a Dream Car bucket that you want to reach in 5 years. But now you're pregnant with baby number three. You need to add a third row to your car, and you need that car ASAP. Your goal will change from being invested to going to cash.

Don't just wait for changes in your circumstances to revisit your Empower Plan. Be proactive and create established check-ins. Remember, people don't *plan* to fail; they fail to plan. Not you!

Set up a schedule that works for you to monitor your investments. If you're invested in funds that automatically rebalance, then twice a year is a good schedule to keep. If you're choosing your investments, you should look to rebalance four times a year. If the markets are volatile, you may want to rebalance more frequently. Choose what works best for you. This schedule needs to be something you can genuinely stick to and a rhythm you naturally gravitate toward.

Put it on your calendar. Put it in your phone. Put it somewhere that will help you stick to it. Plan something fun afterward. For example, know you'll tackle this two times a year on a Saturday morning. Plan a short hike or brunch with friends as a reward afterward. Make it fun. This is not work. This is your life.

The purpose of these check-ins isn't necessarily to prompt change or action. This will continue to raise your awareness around money and the world of investing. It's kind of like when I get allergy shots. I'm highly allergic to pollen. I should star in a Benadryl commercial. The whole point of these shots is to desensitize my body to pollen exposure. That's the purpose of these periodic check-ins. Desensitize yourself to thinking about planning your finances. If you look at this only once a year, it's natural to feel overwhelmed. You are becoming financially fluent, remember? It's a learned skill. You got this!

I've created an Empower Plan Checkup template for you to have handy so when you do these check-ins, you'll know what to consider. You won't be confused about what to evaluate. You'll avoid making panic decisions, such as "My accounts are down, I should probably sell, sell, sell!" You can snag your copy from the digital assets page or create your own. Use this as a template:

Purpose:

Bring awareness to my investments.

Emotional Check-In:

How am I feeling about my current financial situation and investment strategy?

If I'm not feeling great, I can revisit the three-step process to bring myself back.

What kind of support do I need right now to move through this?

What should I take into consideration?

Is the asset allocation of each goal in line with my time frame, risk tolerance, and financial situation? Is the asset allocation similar to what I originally picked?

Do I need to rebalance?

Is my investment automatically rebalancing?

If not, should I sell or buy anything new?

How has the investment performed?

Is my investment up or down?

Date of my next scheduled checkup?

Where is the reminder for my next checkup, e.g., phone, work calendar, etc.?

LIFE HAPPENS AND THAT'S OKAY

There will be times when you mess up or things change that are out of your control. It's okay. Life happens. Your plan will not fall apart overnight. Leave space for forgiveness and fluidity. If life was predictable, I could tell you exactly how much money to save, what to invest in, and when your last day on this earth would be. You'd be able to create the perfect financial plan. We would also be bored every day. Life is ever changing and you along with it. Be kind to yourself throughout this journey.

Here's an example of how *not* to approach your goals. As my daughter Harlow approached her first birthday, I made a commitment. I needed to get back to my pre-pregnancy weight before her birthday. If I couldn't lose the weight by then, I'd never lose it. In that moment, I was completely serious. I put so much pressure on that one thought. Each day, it gained momentum. Holy Sulky Suzie, am I right? I repeated this back to myself and couldn't help but laugh hard, out loud. I convinced myself I was doomed to mom jeans for the rest of my life. That's hysterical. I was setting myself up to fail. I was exercising regularly, eating well, and occasionally indulging in scoops of Ben & Jerry's. I needed more time to lose the weight, but I was on my way. Pushing my goal out did not make me a failure.

Don't fret too much about mistakes. Let's say you spent too much over the last six months. Perhaps you made an emotional decision and sold an investment when you shouldn't have. Forgive yourself. Remember, you are always one decision away from a new attitude. Give yourself a break. Call a loving friend who will support you if you come down too hard on yourself.

I've spent much of my life trying to be in control. At some breaking point, that starts to work against you. I teach my son to take deep breaths when he's frustrated or sad. He can be kicking, screaming, or sobbing. I have to tell him to look into my eyes and take a deep breath with me. I do this a few times until he's able to join in to take at least one deep breath. I have to tell you, every time we're done, I feel better. Taking a moment to let things be what they will be and breathe is all you need to get by. Tomorrow is a new day, and as my favorite president, Abraham Lincoln, famously said, "The best thing about the future is that it comes one day at a time."

KEY TAKEAWAYS

In this chapter, you learned five easy action steps for implementing your Empower Plan. You can also find this in the digital assets as part of your Empower Plan Checklist.

Step 1: Confirm your goals using the Investment Goal Strategy Worksheet:

1. Goal name
2. What will this goal do for you?
3. What is your desired target asset allocation?
4. Why?
5. What is your investment strategy?
6. What will your initial deposit be?
7. What will you contribute biweekly or monthly?
8. What is your SMART goal?

Step 2: Choose an investment firm based on value, product offering, service, and credibility.

Step 3: Open your accounts.

Step 4: Fund your accounts.

Step 5: Automate your contributions and investments.

We also talked about creating a system for monitoring your plan. Set recurring dates on your calendar that you can stick with. Refer to the Empower Plan Checkup Worksheet.

Last, we talked about how to pivot. Give yourself grace, have patience, and be flexible.

CONCLUSION

"We can't become what we need to be by remaining what we are."

—OPRAH WINFREY

Financial empowerment is trending. This topic sparks stimulating conversations among women everywhere. Whether you discuss it over coffee with a close girlfriend or in a room full of ambitious women, the idea that we need a seat at the table is clear. But what happens when those conversations end? When weeks pass by and the enthusiasm starts to wear off, where do you stand? When you're no longer in the company of your lady power squad, what do you do?

Financial empowerment is not how you feel after talking about money. Financial empowerment is the ability to make confident financial decisions—decisions that allow you to build and keep wealth, invest with purpose, and pursue fulfillment. Financial empowerment is earned. Do you want to talk about it or lead us down the road to empowerment?

Let's return to our main characters one final time to see what is possible with financial empowerment.

HAPPY ENDINGS

It's been 7 years since Jessica created her Empower Plan. Jessica is standing around her kitchen island with some girlfriends popping a celebratory bottle of champagne. She officially closed on her first home.

Ashley hikes to the top of a hill near her house overlooking a valley and takes in the moment. She's been working her Empower Plan for 6 years now. She resigned from her job today and is now pursuing her entrepreneurship dream full time. For the first time in her life, she truly believes the sky is the limit.

Mike and Sarah have paid off her student loan debt after intentionally working their Empower Plan for the past 10 years. They are now house hunting for a bigger home. They will soon be a family of four.

Jessica, Ashley, Mike, and Sarah are able to focus on what brings them joy in life. Money and investing are no longer obstacles; they provide solutions. But they didn't start there. They got there by following their Empower Plans.

YOUR EMPOWER PLAN

You, too, can have the lifestyle you want now and in the future by following the steps of your Empower Plan. Remember, people don't plan to fail; they fail to plan. Not you. You got this!

Here's a recap of everything you've learned.

PHASE 1: BUILD A FOUNDATION FOR FINANCIAL EMPOWERMENT

In Phase 1, you learned how to build a rock-solid financial foundation so you can become financially empowered on your own.

You stripped away all ego and got honest with your bad self. You examined your childhood money culture to better understand your money mindset and explored how your emotions influence your financial decisions today. You learned about the most common money blind spots that hold people back from reaching the next level with their finances. You uncovered your own emotional and mental roadblocks and learned an easy three-step process to overcome them: acknowledge the thought, reframe your thinking, and move through it.

You gained greater clarity on what you want out of life. You created intentional financial goals and explored why these goals are important and the impact they will have on your life.

Then you took stock of your current financial situation, learning where and what you spend each month, so you could better map out where you're going. You became a master of your debt and credit. You learned how to organize and prioritize your debt to create a payoff strategy that fits into your lifestyle, and you learned how to build and maintain a high credit score.

PHASE 2: LEARN THE INVESTING ESSENTIALS AND EXPLORE STRATEGIES

With a strong financial foundation in place, you started Phase 2, where you began learning core investing concepts. You learned why and how we invest our money. You learned what roles stocks, bonds, and cash play, and you discovered the importance of asset allocation and diversification.

You learned how to block out the noisy world of the stock market and choose an investment strategy that aligns with your preferences based on your goal's time frame, your risk tolerance, and your current financial situation.

You found out how the retirement landscape has been changing and what this means for you today. You figured out how much you should and could save for retirement, and you created an investment strategy based on your circumstances and made some serious decisions with confidence.

Throughout Phase 2, what was once intimidating and overwhelming became clear. You left this phase walking taller, able to choose a road to your final destination with confidence.

PHASE 3: PUT IT ALL TOGETHER

In the final phase, you put it all together, moving from vague ideas to concrete action. You learned how to turn your goals into reality with the concept of SMART—specific, measurable, achievable, relevant, and timely—goal planning. You played around with the adjustable elements of your financial goals to find the right formula to match your lifestyle and priorities.

Then you learned how to make money moves like a *boss*! You explored how to choose an investment firm to partner with. You set your savings and investments on autopilot and learned how to monitor your financial plan and pivot when life happens and you're knocked off track. You're now well on your way to financial empowerment.

YOUR FUTURE IS WAITING

You are no longer daydreaming about "what if" and "I wish." You wanted an accessible, easy-to-understand resource that could help you become financially empowered, and you got it. Using what you've learned, you'll be able to reach your version of financial freedom. You now have the tools to live a debt-free life, travel the world, provide for your children in a way you didn't think possible, or whatever you desire. You also know how to set yourself up for retirement so when you're older, you will work if you want to, not because you have to. Yes, there is work involved to reach financial freedom, but you are now financially enlightened. You know how to work the steps. You are completely capable of making all this happen for yourself. You're continuing on your financial journey, and like any other skill, you'll use each experience as a building block to greatness.

All that's left now is to take action. Work the Empower Plan. Talk about it. Share it. We will no longer be left behind. Let's grow together. Empowered women empower women.

JOIN OUR COMMUNITY

As you continue on your path to empowerment, know that you are not alone. I invite you to join our community to find support and inspiration. I welcome you to share your experiences with the community because we can all learn from each other. I hope to see you there. Check us out at www.empoweredplanning.com/superpower.

ACKNOWLEDGMENTS

I have to start by thanking my incredible husband, Conrad. From staying up late to hear my ideas for book structure, to listening to me recite random paragraphs that needed fine-tuning, to entertaining the kids outside of the house early Sunday mornings during a pandemic, he had more than a helping hand in getting this book done. Thank you, darling.

Thank you to Simone for encouraging me to do this and wrapping my kids in your love so they wouldn't miss Mom too much. There would be no book without you. I am forever grateful.

An enormous thank-you to my mom and dad for supporting my decisions and standing behind me with pride. Without your support, this book would still just be an idea. I love you!

I am eternally grateful for my children, Holden and Harlow. Their patience and adaptability to a pandemic and mom putting in extra work hours were the focus of my motivation. Holden wrote a book since all he heard about for months was that I couldn't play because I was writing a book. Harlow greeted me with cuddles and smiles. They gave me the inspiration to follow my dreams.

I am so grateful for my friends, who played a special role in helping me complete this book. To Brad Finkelstein, who listened to me talk countless times about how hard it was to write a book and who sincerely reminded me time and time again that most things worth doing aren't easy.

To Katie D'Amato, who had more confidence in me than I did when I told her I was going to write a book. Her friendship made me stand taller and pushed me to get this book off the ground.

To Alisha Ochoa, who would take random phone calls, walks on the beach, or virtual coffee dates for book therapy.

I am forever grateful to Maggie Larson, who always pushed and encouraged me to be me. She reminded me that it's okay to be a mom, run a business, and write a book. Not just her words but her actions in her own life lit an internal fire inside of me to finish this book.

A wholehearted thank-you to Steve Mastroianni, my mentor and friend. His candid guidance, humor, and toughness helped me write the best version of this book. I would still be editing if it wasn't for his not-so-gentle (*wink wink*) shove to the finish line.

Lindsay Moore, who held my business down so I could write this book, you are an amazing lady!

Having the idea to write a book and actually writing a book are two different things. Thank you to Miles Rote for introducing me to Scribe. He knew I had a story to tell and believed I could do it when it was just an idea. He laid out the path and challenged me to hop on it.

To everyone on the Scribe team for helping me bring this all to life. A special thanks to Hal and Emily for showing up every week and guiding me to the finish line, to Kelsey for truly seeing me in my words, and to Mikey for being my cheerleader!

ABOUT THE AUTHOR

SHINOBU HINDERT is a CERTIFIED FINANCIAL PLANNER™ professional, money expert, and creator of Empowered Planning, LLC. She spent the first half of her career working for some of the largest financial institutions in the United States, including Smith Barney and Fidelity Investments. As a financial adviser, she created personalized financial plans for high-networth individuals all across the country, overseeing more than $350 million in client assets.

Now Shinobu has taken all her knowledge and created a simple, proven method for teaching personal finance. She has delivered over five hundred live workshops covering a wide range of topics, from budgeting to estate planning. Her goal is to simplify the complex world of investing and empower women everywhere to reach financial freedom.